Standards for Supporting Crop-related Livelihoods in Emergencies

2022 EDITION

Practical Action Publishing Ltd
25 Albert Street, Rugby, Warwickshire, CV21 2SG, UK
www.practicalactionpublishing.com

A catalogue record for this book is available from the British Library.

A catalogue record for this book has been requested from the Library of Congress.

ISBN 978-1-78853-239-6 Paperback
ISBN 978-1-78853-241-9 Electronic book

Citation: SEADS (2022), *Standards for Supporting Crop-related Livelihoods in Emergencies*, Rugby, UK: Practical Action Publishing. http://dx.doi.org/10.3362/9781788532419

Since 1974, Practical Action Publishing has published and disseminated books and information in support of international development work throughout the world. Practical Action Publishing is a trading name of Practical Action Publishing Ltd (Company Reg. No. 1159018), the wholly owned publishing company of Practical Action. Practical Action Publishing trades only in support of its parent charity objectives and any profits are covenanted back to Practical Action (Charity Reg. No. 247257, Group VAT Registration No. 880 9924 76).

The views and opinions in this publication are those of the author and do not represent those of Practical Action Publishing Ltd or its parent charity Practical Action.

Reasonable efforts have been made to publish reliable data and information, but the authors and publisher cannot assume responsibility for the validity of all materials or for the consequences of their use.

Cover and text design by Jessica Haswell
Cover photo shows Fouriesburg, South Africa. Credit: Adalia Botha
Typesetting by River Valley Technologies
Edited by Kate Murphy

PRAISE FOR THIS BOOK

"A clear and concise yet comprehensive guide to deliver impactful and high-quality agricultural interventions in emergencies. The practical tools and external resources presented here are valuable additions, while the focus on participatory and people-centered approaches is highly relevant. This guide is also a good reminder of aspects that may be overlooked during the planning and implementation phases of an emergency response. Overall, a great resource for our work in the humanitarian sector."

Jo Burton, Head of Economic Security Unit, International Committee of the Red Cross, Switzerland

"This handbook was produced by bringing together the many years of experience of those implementing humanitarian interventions to support crop-related livelihoods, many in very difficult contexts. The result is a very well-presented and welcome handbook that will centralize farmers' needs and priorities and local crop production systems to enable quality, well-designed, and appropriate humanitarian responses. The responses developed with the handbook will ultimately support both farmers impacted by crises as well as those who are part of the wider crop production system, such as seed suppliers and agricultural service providers, for better recovery after a crisis."

David Traynor, Agricultural Advisor, Concern Worldwide

"Evidence-based, livelihoods-based, and rights-based—exactly what is needed to guide emergency response to smallholder crop producers hit by crisis."

Pepijn Schreinemachers, Senior Scientist, World Vegetable Center, Thailand

"The SEADS Handbook will be a valuable tool and input that will allow the construction of contingency plans with a focus on livelihoods, which will be prepared with specific, systematized, and tested activities for the recovery of livelihoods in the affected areas. In addition, SEADS has a strong commitment to the Core Humanitarian Standards, a highly-valued approach for the coordination of humanitarian assistance in our country."

Tania Carias, Emergency Preparedness and Capacity Strengthening Specialist, World Food Program Honduras

"A delightful book full of essential information that would be an added value for all active stakeholders in the agriculture sector of a conflict area such as the Gaza Strip. The number of details and sequence of the presentation show that considerable efforts were invested in this book for the greater benefit of the agriculture sector and specifically for supporting agricultural livelihood during and after emergencies. The SEADS Handbook is an important tool for decision makers, helping them to coordinate their efforts and interventions to reach quickly and effectively the vulnerable and affected farmers."

Hani Al Ramlawi, Programs and Projects Coordinator, The Agricultural Development Association, Gaza

"In Bangladesh, agriculture extension services provide preparedness, emergency, recovery and development assistance to crop producers. SEADS will provide thoughtful consideration by policymakers involved in agricultural extension management systems, and will mark new horizons for how our services respond to crop-related crisis."

Md. Abu Sayem, PhD Fellow, Department of Agricultural Extension, Hajee Mohammad Danesh Science and Technology University, Dinajpur, Bangladesh

CONTENTS

LIST OF FIGURES AND TABLES

SEADS: Minimum Standards for Supporting Crop-related Livelihoods in Emergencies

Agriculture is the sustaining livelihood for millions of people across the world, and crop-related support is an important component of crisis response. SEADS is a set of international principles and minimum standards that support humanitarians to design, implement, and evaluate crop-related crisis responses.

SEADS minimum standards are based on global evidence of impact from crop-related responses, local perspectives, technical expertise, a global public consultation, and regional simulation events. SEADS is collaborative and inclusive; you can provide feedback at any time on the content of this Handbook through the Humanitarian Standards Partnership (HSP) website.

SEADS takes a livelihoods approach to crop-related crisis response. This perspective means that the SEADS minimum standards address not only immediate crisis response, but also early recovery, links to development, and consideration of crisis and climate trends affecting communities that rely heavily on crops. SEADS also promotes ways to provide support during crises to systems and services that are needed to enable post-disaster recovery.

CHAPTER 1:
HOW TO USE THIS HANDBOOK

Annex A: Glossary contains definitions of some of the technical terms used in SEADS.

What is SEADS?

The SEADS Handbook (SEADS) is a set of international principles and minimum standards that support those responding to a humanitarian crisis to design, implement, and evaluate crop-related crisis responses.

The SEADS principles and minimum standards guide decision making and allow you to:

- determine if a crop-related response is appropriate, necessary, and feasible
- prioritize which crop-related response area may achieve livelihood objectives given the context
- track alignment of your projects with minimum standards
- measure impact from crop-related crisis response.

Using the SEADS principles and minimum standards will strengthen the quality of crop-related crisis response and support the saving of lives by saving livelihoods before, during, and after a crisis.

SEADS is not a how-to manual for implementing a crop-related crisis response; therefore it should be used alongside other resources referred to in each chapter.

Although many crop producers and agro-pastoralists practice mixed farming, growing crops alongside other productive activities, SEADS does not provide technical guidance on livestock, fisheries, aquaculture, or forestry. Specific guidance on these is available elsewhere; for instance, in the *Livestock Emergency Guidelines and Standards* and the *Fisheries and Aquaculture International Guidelines* (FAO 2021).

Who should use SEADS?

Anyone who is involved in crop-related crisis response can use SEADS. It will be particularly useful for people who provide preparedness, emergency, recovery, and development assistance in areas where crop production contributes to livelihoods. That includes humanitarian actors, bilateral and multilateral organizations, non-governmental organizations (NGO), governments, community-based organizations, and civil society organizations.

It will also be useful for policy makers and decision makers in donor and government agencies, whose funding and implementation decisions affect crisis response.

How should I use SEADS?

Read Chapters 1–3 first. Those chapters explain critical concepts that underpin SEADS and allow you to implement an effective response.

Once you are familiar with the fundamental concepts on which SEADS is based, read the minimum standards chapters, starting at Chapter 4: Initial Assessment for Crop-related Crisis Response. The information and practical tools in Chapter 4 will direct you to one or more technical response options (Chapters 5–7). Chapters 5–7 provide tools, such as decision trees, timing tables, and tables of advantages and disadvantages, to help you achieve the minimum standards.

Regardless of which technical response option/s you use, you should read and apply Chapter 8: Impact-oriented Monitoring and Evaluation which describes the minimum standards for impact-oriented monitoring and evaluation. All the minimum standards chapters provide you with key actions and guidance notes for you to design, implement, and evaluate crop-related crisis response.

Annex A: Glossary contains definitions of technical terms that are used throughout SEADS.

At the end of each chapter you'll find a list of recommended reading that contains additional information, explanations, and tools. Annex C: References contains a bibliography of the references that are cited in each chapter.

Figure 1.1 shows the relationship between the chapters and annexes in SEADS.

Figure 1.1: Steps for using SEADS effectively

1 *Read Chapters 1–3*

Chapter 1: How to Use this Handbook
Chapter 2: The Scope and Approach of SEADS
Chapter 3: SEADS Principles

2 *Use SEADS minimum standards to design, implement, and evaluate crop-related responses*

Chapter 4: Initial Assessment for Crop-related Crisis Response
Chapter 5: Seed and Seed Systems
Chapter 6: Tools, Equipment, and Other Non-seed Inputs
Chapter 7: Crop-related Infrastructure
Chapter 8: Impact-oriented Monitoring and Evaluation

3 *Use annexes to inform your understanding of the standards*

Annex A: Glossary
Annex B: Elements of Team Competency
Annex C: References
Annex D: Acknowledgments and Contributors

SEADS is available in print and as a downloadable PDF on the SEADS website. SEADS is a member of the Humanitarian Standards Partnership (HSP), so you can also use SEADS on the HSP website or on your mobile device with the HSP app. Both the Interactive Handbook platform and the HSP app allow you to provide feedback on SEADS at any time.

What is the structure of each SEADS minimum standard?

The standard

The standard is a qualitative statement applicable in any crisis situation that is a general description, stating the minimum actions and outcomes to be achieved in any crisis.

Key actions

Practical steps to attain the standard. They may not be applicable in all contexts, so select the most relevant for your situation.

Guidance notes

Additional information to support the key actions, with cross-references to SEADS principles, the *Sphere Handbook* (including the Protection Principles and the Core Humanitarian Standard) (Sphere Association 2018), other HSP standards, and other SEADS minimum standards.

Key process indicators

Key process indicators allow you to monitor adherence to the standard. Suggested indicators are listed in Appendix 8.5. Chapter 8 includes impact indicators that seek to measure the impact of any crop-related crisis response against the SEADS livelihood objectives.

Note that minimum standards may not always be achievable in the short term, particularly if it is the first time that you are considering them. However, continuous consideration of minimum standards across all crop-related responses in all crisis contexts can bring you closer to consistent achievement over time.

Supplementary resources

SEADS is supplemented by:

- the *SEADS Evidence Database*
- recommended reading lists at the end of most chapters
- a series of case studies on the SEADS website https://seads-standards.org/casestudies

When should I use SEADS?

You should use SEADS whenever you suspect that crops may be important to the past, current, or future livelihoods of people affected by crisis. At the moment you realize crops may be, or may have been, important to livelihoods, pick up SEADS and follow the steps in Figure 1.1.

A crop-related crisis response will not be suitable in all contexts. Conduct an initial assessment to determine whether a crop-related response is appropriate, necessary, and feasible. Then use response identification tools to prioritize crop-related response areas that may achieve livelihood objectives given the context. Use the minimum standards in Chapter 4 to guide you through these two processes and determine which, if any, crop-related response areas are suitable.

You can also use SEADS if you find yourself in the midst of a crop-related response and you want to know how to strengthen it or how to ensure that your response has an impact on the livelihoods of people affected by crisis.

CHAPTER 2:
THE SCOPE AND APPROACH OF SEADS

> Annex A: Glossary contains definitions of some of the technical terms used in SEADS.

Why is crop-related crisis response important?

Millions of people around the world who are vulnerable to crisis rely heavily on crop production to support their livelihoods. Currently, 40% of the global poor live in economies affected by fragility, conflict, and violence. That number is expected to rise to 67% in the next decade (World Bank 2021). Most very poor people live in rural areas, and many of them produce their own food and income through agriculture production (World Bank 2016). People produce food for themselves, their communities, and the food supply chain, and they generate income if they sell food they have produced. Support for crop-based livelihoods in a crisis can protect and rebuild this essential activity and can prevent more extreme food insecurity. Provision of essential crop-related inputs ensures continued food production in the short and medium term. Protection, provision, and rehabilitation of crop-related infrastructure and equipment ensure future production and make people more resilient to crises.

By protecting and rebuilding crop-based livelihoods before, during, and after a crisis, crop-related crisis response mitigates the impacts of the crisis by contributing to a sustainable food supply and potential source of income for the very poor. Crop-related crisis responses can also act as a form of social protection, helping smallholders and their families cope with crisis and shocks by reducing food losses and by supporting a return to or an increase in food production.

During a crisis, crop production and many associated services that make crop production possible may be disrupted, making it more difficult for people to meet their food and income needs. A crop-related crisis response is important because it can keep people from starving, from adopting negative coping mechanisms, and from migrating. It offers them assistance that can help reduce the impact of future crises. It has the potential to support a more sustainable use of natural resources and to enhance market system linkages and viability.

What is a crop-related crisis response?

A crop-related crisis response is the actions taken by state and non-state actors before, during, and after a crisis to support the livelihoods of crop producers and associated systems, services, policies, and markets.

The specific crop-related crisis response required depends on the context (emergency, operational, agricultural) and the objectives of the action. Crop-related crisis responses can include preparing crop producers and their communities for future shocks and rebuilding livelihoods after a crisis. Responses that are well designed and implemented can:

- improve food security and nutrition
- generate income and improve household economies
- enhance the sustainable use and management of natural resources
- support social capital and networks
- provide institutional assistance for early warning and anticipatory action and ensure appropriate preparation before a crisis occurs
- support actors along the value-chain to ensure crop production, storage, and marketing
- coordinate between development and humanitarian actors for effective decision making
- avoid or lessen the risk of the worst forms of child labor, child marriage, sexual exploitation, and/or family separation
- ensure appropriate organizational skills before a crisis.

Which crisis-affected people can benefit from SEADS?

SEADS covers the hundreds of millions of people around the world whose livelihoods are supported by crop production, including millions of state and non-state actors who provide essential production and post-harvest assistance services to crop producers. The SEADS principles and minimum standards will primarily benefit those who have experienced loss of life or property or for whom basic human rights are not accessible and who require crop-related humanitarian assistance to support their livelihoods, such as:

- smallholder or subsistence crop producers
- home and market gardeners
- landless and displaced crop producers
- farm laborers.

SEADS will also benefit state and non-state service providers who enable the crop-based livelihoods of those affected by crisis, such as:

- seed producers
- non-seed input manufacturers and sellers
- post-harvest processors
- extension agents
- financial service providers
- producer organizations
- transporters.

What crops and crises does SEADS cover?

SEADS targets the production of different crops in different settings. SEADS principles and minimum standards apply to:

- field or garden crops for own consumption or as a livelihood activity
- different agro-ecological zones around the world
- crop production in rural, peri-urban, and urban settings
- crop production practiced by displaced people, including those living in camps
- rapid-onset, slow-onset, and complex crises, and the short-term or longer-term responses associated with each.

What approach does SEADS take to crop-related response?

SEADS is:

- evidence based
- livelihoods based
- rights based.

Evidence-based approach

SEADS is guided by a systematic review of over 250 evaluations of crop-related responses in humanitarian crises. The review focused on livelihoods, food security, and nutrition impacts of the main types of crop-related crisis response, including seeds, tools, and other inputs; producer training; pest and disease control; and market support (SEADS 2021).

The results of this evidence review are in the *SEADS Evidence Database*. If you are aware of additional evidence, you can submit it through our website.

Livelihoods-based approach

SEADS is based on a livelihoods approach because crop-related crisis responses support livelihoods. This approach fits within the concept of "saving lives and livelihoods," which is widely recognized by the international humanitarian community as a core aim of humanitarian programming. This approach also reflects learning on the importance of resilience; if livelihoods are resilient, households and communities are more able to prepare for and recover from future shocks. Livelihoods are the capabilities, assets (including both material and non-material resources), and activities required to make a living. In addition to supporting food production for own consumption, livelihood impacts are the reason that crop-related crisis response should be undertaken. SEADS livelihood objectives define the desired livelihood impacts of any crop-related crisis response.

Support to existing local service providers and markets, wherever this is feasible and relevant, is an important aspect of livelihoods-based crisis response and applies to all types of crisis. SEADS aims to support these local systems to enable recovery and long-term development. SEADS Principle 1: Use livelihoods-based programming provides additional details on factors that are critical to livelihood analysis for crop-related crisis response.

Table 2.1 sets out the three SEADS livelihood objectives.

Table 2.1: SEADS livelihood objectives

Objective 1	Objective 2	Objective 3
To provide immediate livelihood benefits to people affected by crisis	To protect crop-related livelihoods of people affected by crisis	To rebuild or support crop-related production, infrastructure, and systems to ensure livelihoods for people affected by crisis

These livelihood objectives and the SEADS livelihoods-based approach mirror those in the *Livestock Emergency Guidelines and Standards* (LEGS). Crop-related crisis response should meet one or more livelihood objectives.

Objective 1 recognizes that people may require rapid assistance during a crisis to produce crops in line with their normal livelihood practices. Examples include: supplying tools or equipment to harvest crops (which would otherwise go unharvested); providing rapid market access to enable crops to be sold; facilitating access to transportation so a producer can get to the market to buy seed.

Objective 2 recognizes the need to maintain pre-production, production, post-production, and marketing activities so livelihoods can be re-established after the crisis. Such actions may not provide direct benefits to people during the crisis. For example, organizations can support repair of a storage warehouse so people will be able to safely store and sell their harvested crops in the future.

Objective 3 recognizes the need to support people's resilience to future shocks or to rebuild where substantial losses of infrastructure and systems have occurred. For example, organizations can support community-based seed producers to breed context-relevant varieties to promote continuity of production, or participatory varietal selection, or early access to already released appropriate varieties.

Working toward livelihood objectives will improve the quality of crop-related crisis responses and the likelihood that such responses will have an impact on livelihoods. The objectives have an equal capacity to have an impact on crop-based livelihoods, but people may feel that impact at different times. Immediate livelihood benefits could be achieved within approximately 30 days (Objective 1). The benefits of protecting, rebuilding, or supporting crop-related livelihoods are not likely to be felt before the end of one cropping cycle and are more likely to be felt after two or three cycles (Objectives 2 and 3). Expectations of exactly when people will feel livelihood impacts from assistance are context specific. Chapter 8: Impact-oriented Monitoring and Evaluation provides guidance on participatory impact evaluations that measure livelihood impacts during or at the end of a project.

Chapter 4: Initial Assessment for Crop-related Crisis Response provides details on prioritizing livelihood objectives and identifying response areas appropriate for each livelihood objective.

Rights-based approach

A rights-based approach encourages participation, empowerment, accountability, and non-discrimination when delivering crisis response or development programs, including crop-related responses. SEADS principles and minimum standards reflect this rights-based approach.

SEADS supports crop-related crisis responses that take steps to ensure:

The right to food

Crop producers have a right to assistance to protect and rebuild the livelihoods that provide food for themselves and their communities. The right to food is an inclusive right; it is realized when food is available, accessible, and adequate. Availability relates to food availability from natural resources or in a market. Accessibility requires economic and physical access to food. Adequacy relates to dietary needs, food safety, and cultural acceptability.

The right to life with dignity

Many impacts of disasters are directly borne by smallholders (FAO 2017). Crop producers have a right to assistance to maintain a dignified standard of living that supports their families. The process of active community participation in crisis response (see SEADS Principle 2: Use a participatory approach in all aspects of crisis response) is an important aspect of supporting the dignity of crisis-affected crop producers.

SEADS and communities affected by conflict

SEADS is aligned with the humanitarian-development-peace (HDP) nexus. Millions of smallholder or subsistence crop producers, home and market gardeners , and landless crop producers are affected by prolonged and severe conflict. Crop-related responses often take place in fragile and conflict-prone areas (Tschunkert & Delgado 2022); today, most emergency agriculture funding and effort is channeled to complex crises. In addition, the incidence of complex crises in middle-income countries is increasing and with it the need for additional crop-related humanitarian assistance.

SEADS principles and minimum standards provide numerous opportunities to work in the HDP nexus. The HDP nexus focuses on the work needed to coherently address people's vulnerability before, during, and after crises. This nexus is becoming increasingly important to consider in humanitarian response, as humanitarian funding in conflict areas grows.

Crop-related crisis responses support coherent HDP approaches by:

- gathering livelihoods-based assessment data that consider environmental, political, and sociocultural trends that may affect crop producers' ability to engage in the essential activity of food production
- identifying and addressing issues that ensure crop production leads to livelihood benefits that can be felt after the crisis has passed
- focusing on preparedness for upcoming crop seasons
- strengthening and supporting local seed, tool, equipment, and infrastructure systems and related services that can improve social cohesion and prevent future conflicts
- providing flexible funds or "crisis modifiers" within development areas prone to natural disasters or recurring conflict, enabling crisis planning and response to be integrated into long-term development strategies.

What types of crisis can affect crop producers?

SEADS categorizes crises as slow onset, rapid onset, and complex. Table 2.2 describes the three types of crisis and their impacts on production and livelihoods; impacts on production trigger gradual worsening of human food security and livelihoods. Some types of crisis may also be categorized as chronic if the events or phases of the event repeat themselves with no or limited return to the previous conditions.

Table 2.2: Slow-onset, rapid-onset, and complex crises have different impacts on crop production

Type and characteristics	Impact on production and livelihoods
Slow-onset crisis	
Gradual, increasing stress on livelihoods over many months until a crisis is declared	Crop area coverage decreases, and crop performance gradually worsens in early phases of a slow-onset crisis, particularly in annual or horticultural crops
Can be a multiyear event	
Specific geographical areas are known to be at risk, so there is some level of predictability	Crop loss is excessive and worsens in later phases of a slow-onset crisis

...continued

Early response is often non-existent even though early-warning systems exist

Examples include drought, plant pests (such as fall armyworm), plant diseases (such as wheat rust, anthracnose, head smut), parasitic weeds (such as *Striga hermonthica*), pollution, and salinization

Market prices rise due to limited supply

Reduced product quality generates lower prices and therefore reduced income

Rapid-onset crisis

Occurs with little or no warning, although specific geographical areas often have known risks

When an alarm is given, it tends to be with little notice

Most impact occurs immediately or within hours or days

In the immediate aftermath, recovery can take days (for example, receding floods), months, or years (for example, an earthquake or volcanic eruption)

Examples include flood, earthquake, typhoon, volcanic eruption, tsunami, and pest or disease outbreaks

Displacement affects labor availability

Movement of goods and people needed to produce crops is restricted

Crop loss is excessive and rapid during the initial event

Market prices rise due to limited supply

Infrastructure and physical assets are immediately damaged or destroyed

Purchasing power collapses

Markets close due to infrastructure loss, border closures, quarantine, lockdown, or conflict

Complex crisis

Associated with protracted political instability and/or internal or external armed conflict

Time frame is usually years to decades

Displacement affects labor availability

Crop loss is excessive and low production can become chronic

A slow-onset or a rapid-onset crisis can also occur simultaneously, worsening the impacts of the ongoing complex crisis

Examples include ongoing conflict with drought (such as in Sudan), civil war (such as in the Central African Republic and Syria), and terrorism with drought and displacement (such as in northern Nigeria)

New types of complex crisis can emerge (such as COVID-19)

Infrastructure and services to support production are damaged or destroyed

Markets are disrupted on a wide scale

Access to productive assets is disrupted. This situation may be temporary in the case of an internal displacement or long term in the case of significant physical damage to or contamination of land and infrastructure

State and non-state services deteriorate over time

How does a crisis impact the livelihoods of crop producers?

A crisis impacts people's livelihoods, food security, and nutrition. For crop producers the severity of these impacts varies, depending on the nature of the crisis and when in the agriculture calendar the crisis occurs. In general, a crisis:

- limits crop producers' access to land, infrastructure, financial services, machinery, equipment, labor, or inputs, which delays or prevents time-sensitive tasks, such as planting, weeding, harvesting, or sales
- impedes crop growth due to factors such as too much water (for example, flooding), not enough water (for example, drought), pollution, volcanic ash, extreme temperatures, or salinization
- physically damages or destroys infrastructure, assets, stored inputs and harvests, or crops
- disrupts supply chains and their associated markets, leading to loss of or reduced access to critical crop production inputs, such as seeds and fertilizer
- causes the collapse of state and non-state extension, research, and marketing services due to displacement, lockdown, or destruction of equipment and infrastructure
- increases competition for limited natural resources required for crop production.

The increased frequency of severe weather-related events and the emergence of new civil conflicts pose significant challenges to smallholder households from loss of production and income. According to FAO (2017), natural hazards and disasters have doubled in frequency since 1992.

A complex crisis—typically prolonged and driven by political instability and conflict—also poses severe challenges to crop producers. Livelihood impacts from such a crisis can be worsened by natural disasters and underlying contexts of poverty, climate change, and other factors (CFS 2015). In a complex crisis, crop producers, whether they remain in their homes or are displaced, face unpredictable and often cyclical patterns of restricted production, reduced access to food and income, malnutrition, and poverty.

Crop-based livelihoods are also under continuous threat from pest and disease outbreaks. Some, such as desert locust, fall armyworm, and cassava mosaic disease, cause direct damage to crops. Others have less direct but significant impacts. For example, the COVID-19 pandemic and efforts to control it resulted in devastating movement and trade restrictions. These prevented migrant farm workers from accessing jobs and income, reduced food production in communities dependent on that labor, and prevented producers and consumers from accessing markets (FAO 2021).

Examples of crises and impacts

Slow-onset crisis: Ethiopia

La Niña- and *El Niño-*related weather events triggered severe rain shortages in the southern highlands and the lowlands of southeastern Ethiopia in 2008, 2009, and 2010, which culminated in the 2011 drought. Rainfed crop production for maize, sorghum, and teff was affected in both planting seasons. The main teff-producing zones in the region were among the most affected, most notably North Shewa, West Shewa, Southwest Shewa, and East Gojjam. Coffee plantations were significantly affected, and key coffee-producing zones in the Oromia and Southern Nations, Nationals, and Peoples' Region (Illubabor, Kelem, and Keffa) recorded high losses. Finally, the production of key staple crops, such as sorghum and maize, was strongly affected in Amhara and Dire Dawa Regions as well as in the Somali Region, especially in Jijiga. Area coverage was reduced, and crop performance was poor or failed completely. Lost production and the related loss of income accounted for 96% of all impact. Physical damage from the drought caused fewer impacts (only 4%) in Ethiopia during this time (FAO 2017).

Rapid-onset crisis: Typhoon Haiyan

In 2013, Typhoon Haiyan hit the central Philippines. Its winds were the strongest ever recorded in the country during a cyclone landfall. An estimated 6,300 people died in the cyclone and its immediate aftermath, and 16 million people were affected. Although Typhoon Haiyan struck after the harvest, it caused US$857 million in damage and loss of perennial crops, primarily coconut, banana, mango, papaya, and pineapple. According to government data, 441,256 hectares of coconut plantations were affected by the typhoon, 40% of which were damaged with no chance of recovery. The high value of coconut plantations, combined with the long time required for coconut trees to become fully productive again (seven years), significantly affected crop-based livelihoods. The loss of annual crops and associated production decreases accounted for 89% of total annual crop damage and loss (FAO 2017).

Complex crisis: Syrian Arab Republic

Since March 2011, the Syrian Arab Republic has experienced both natural disasters and protracted conflict. Violence, displacement, crop destruction, and weather-related events have impacted multiple cropping seasons. Agriculture in Syria contributes an estimated 26% to gross domestic product and is a critical livelihood safety net for 6.7 million Syrians—including those internally displaced—who remain in rural areas. Rural households have been hit particularly hard by the conflict, as agricultural land and assets have been destroyed and access to inputs and markets is limited. From 2011 to 2016, annual crops registered the largest share of lost production, as area cultivated in wheat, barley, cotton, sugar beet, tobacco, lentils, chickpeas, and cotton decreased by 30% on average, and by 50% for irrigated land. Insecurity and the high price of inputs caused 10% of households to stop crop production entirely (FAO 2017).

A new type of crisis: COVID-19

The COVID-19 pandemic has affected virtually all regions of the world. In many low-income countries, while human mortality has been relatively low, the economic and food security impacts of COVID-19 restrictions are comparable with a humanitarian crisis. These restrictions have required people to stay at home. Crop production has been affected directly and indirectly, and COVID-19 restrictions have disrupted the movement of food and labor from farms to markets and to people's homes.

Food prices have increased by as much as 53.5% in Myanmar, 38.5% in Mozambique, 25% in Nigeria, and 20% in Guatemala (FAO Data Lab 2021).

Markets have been closed or their hours reduced, and public transportation shut down, affecting physical access to food. In Mozambique in July 2020, 30% of the population reported challenges in access to markets (OCHA 2020). This limited mobility and shifts in consumer demand due to movement restrictions led to a loss of income for crop producers who were unable to sell their produce.

Disruptions in local, national, and global supply chains have compromised producers' access to inputs, resources, and services they need to continue producing and selling food. For example, in Kenya smallholders who export flowers, vegetables, nuts, coffee, and cocoa were affected by cancelled freight operations and border restrictions. In Bangladesh, breakdowns in the transportation system led to the dumping of perishable food products and dramatic price reductions for on-farm selling (FAO 2021).

With the onset of the pandemic in Haiti, the overall percentage of households owning agricultural equipment declined from 48% in January 2020 to 10% in February 2021 as they sold off their productive assets in an attempt to cope with the worsening economic and food security situation (IMPEL 2022). Movement restrictions also caused disruptions in harvesting due to lack of seasonal labor as well as in planting due to a lack of seed or fertilizer (OCHA 2020).

What are the SEADS foundations?

SEADS is based on established humanitarian foundations, specifically:

- the Humanitarian Charter
- Protection Principles
- the Core Humanitarian Standard
- the *Sphere Handbook*.

SEADS recognizes and commits to these fundamental elements in all humanitarian contexts for all crop-related crisis responses, as illustrated in Figure 2.1. SEADS is also aligned with HSP member standards.

Figure 2.1: SEADS principles and minimum standards use humanitarian foundations and livelihoods, evidence, and rights-based approaches to support the quality and accountability of crop-related crisis response

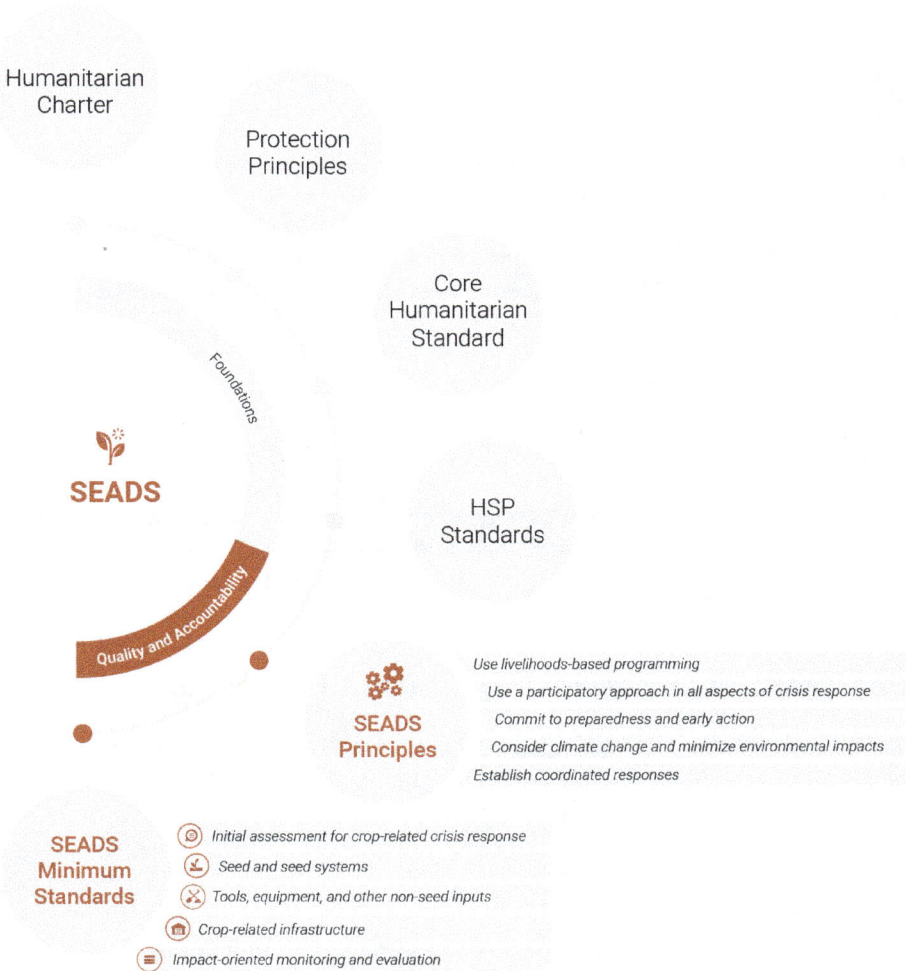

The Humanitarian Charter

The Humanitarian Charter (Sphere Association 2018) expresses a shared conviction of humanitarian organizations that all people affected by crisis have a right to receive protection and assistance to ensure the basic conditions for life with dignity. The Charter provides the ethical and legal backdrop to the Protection Principles, the Core Humanitarian Standard, and Sphere and the HSP.

Protection Principles

The *Sphere Handbook* recognizes four Protection Principles that apply to all humanitarian action and all humanitarian actors:

Protection Principle 1: Enhance people's safety, dignity, and rights, and avoid exposing them to further harm.

Protection Principle 2: Ensure people's access to impartial assistance according to need and without discrimination.

Protection Principle 3: Assist people to recover from the physical and psychological effects of threatened or actual violence, coercion, or deliberate deprivation.

Protection Principle 4: Help people to claim their rights.

The Core Humanitarian Standard

The Core Humanitarian Standard includes nine commitments that aid organization and individuals make to affected people and communities. These commitments contribute to improving the quality and accountability of their activities (see Figure 2.2).

Sphere and the Humanitarian Standards Partnership

The *Sphere Handbook* sets out global minimum standards for humanitarian actions. Sphere acts as the foundation for other humanitarian standards initiatives, including SEADS, which together comprise the Humanitarian Standards Partnership (HSP):

- *Sphere Handbook*
- *Minimum Standards for Child Protection in Humanitarian Action (CPMS)*
- *Livestock Emergency Guidelines and Standards (LEGS)*
- *Minimum Economic Recovery Standards (MERS)*
- *Minimum Standards for Education: Preparedness, Response, Recovery (INEE Minimum Standards)*
- *Minimum Standard for Market Analysis (MISMA)*
- *Humanitarian Inclusion Standards for Older People and People with Disabilities (HIS)*
- *Minimum Standards for Camp Management (CAMP)*
- *Standards for Supporting Crop-related Livelihoods in Emergencies (SEADS).*

Figure 2.2: The Core Humanitarian Standard

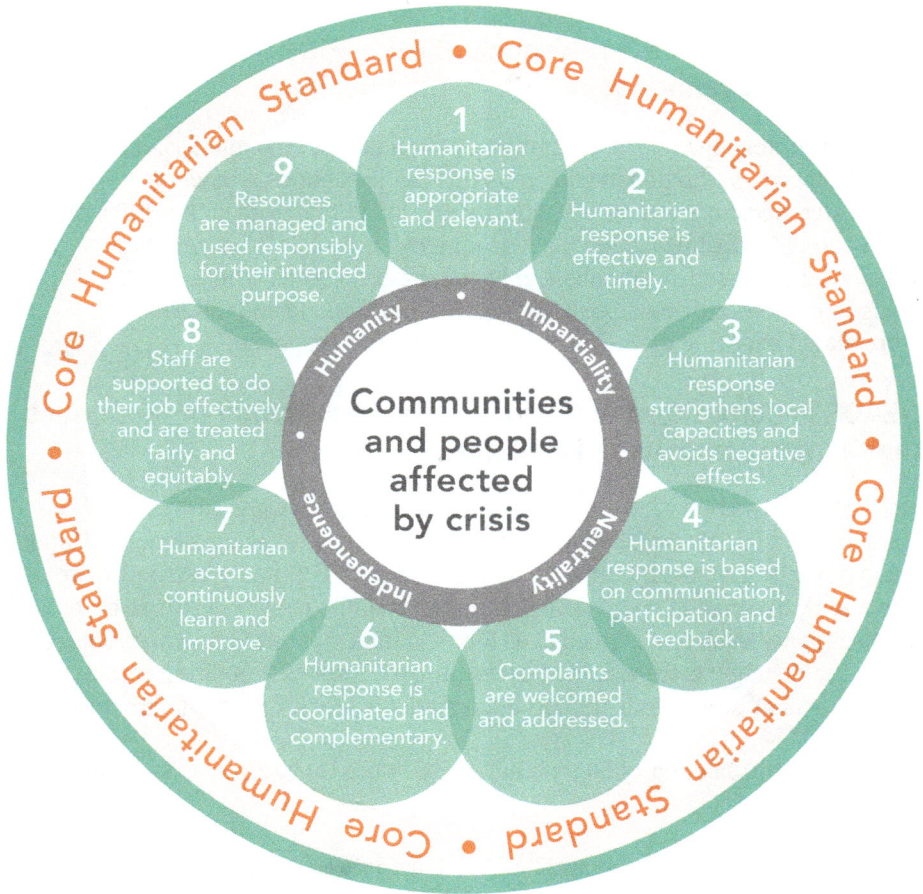

The main aims of the HSP are to improve the quality and accountability of humanitarian action across different sectors and to support users to develop harmonized approaches in the application of standards. The HSP organizes joint training opportunities, research initiatives, and outreach activities. It also runs advocacy activities calling for an increased application of humanitarian standards.

How does SEADS fit in humanitarian response?

SEADS reinforces the relevance of other HSP initiatives to crop-based livelihoods

SEADS reinforces the relevance of the HSP standards to the millions of people affected by crisis who depend on crops for their livelihoods. Frequent cross-references to the *Sphere Handbook* and other initiatives in the HSP indicate when non-crop specific issues, such as employment, child labor, or livestock, may influence crop-based livelihoods and should be considered. These cross-references provide crucial links between protecting and rebuilding crop-related assets and other areas of humanitarian response.

SEADS is committed to quality and accountability of responses that support crop-based livelihoods

The *Core Humanitarian Standard on Quality and Accountability* (CHS) states that accountability is "the process of using power responsibly, taking account of, and being held accountable by, different stakeholders, and primarily those who are affected by exercise of such power." A commitment to the CHS is made at the organizational level, so it applies to all humanitarian responses that an organization supports, including crop-related crisis responses . Table 2.3 outlines specific components of SEADS that support accountability to the CHS commitments.

Table 2.3: SEADS supports alignment with the Core Humanitarian Standard

Core Humanitarian Standard commitments and quality criteria	Elements of SEADS that support alignment with the CHS
1. Communities and people affected by crisis receive assistance appropriate and relevant to their needs Quality criterion: Humanitarian response is appropriate and relevant	Use of a participatory approach during initial assessment and response identification (SEADS Principle 2) supports more appropriate and relevant assistance Use of minimum standards on assessment and planning ensures suitability (Minimum Standards 5.1, 6.1, 7.1)

Use of minimum standards on choice, quality, and technical specifications of crop-related assistance ensures suitability (Minimum Standards 5.4, 5.5, 6.4, 6.5, 7.2, 7.3, 8.2)

Use of minimum standards for monitoring and impact evaluation determines livelihood impacts (Chapter 8)

2. Communities and people affected by crisis have access to the humanitarian assistance they need at the right time

Quality criterion: Humanitarian response is effective and timely

Use of SEADS Principle 3 focuses on a timely response

Use of timing tables ensures that crop-related assistance aligns with agriculture calendars (Tables 5.5, 6.5, and 7.4)

Use of minimum standards for response identification and timing ensures that crop-related assistance considers critical aspects of timing in response identification (Minimum Standards 4.4, 5.2, 6.2, 7.3)

Use of minimum standards for monitoring and impact evaluation determines livelihood impacts; these impacts reflect the timeliness of response (Chapter 8)

3. Communities and people affected by crisis are not negatively affected and are more prepared, resilient, and less at risk as a result of humanitarian action

Quality criterion: Humanitarian response strengthens local capacities and avoids negative effects

Working toward achievement of SEADS livelihood objectives (Table 2.1) improves the likelihood that crop-related response will support livelihoods that are more prepared and less at risk

SEADS Principle 1 recommends working with local actors, systems, and services where possible

...continued

4. Communities and people affected by crisis know their rights and entitlements, have access to information, and participate in decisions that affect them

Quality criterion: Humanitarian response is based on communication, participation, and feedback

SEADS Principle 2 emphasizes community involvement in project design, implementation, and evaluation

Chapter 4 emphasizes community participation in initial assessment and response identification

Use of community participation in monitoring and evaluation improves understanding of impacts (Minimum Standard 8.1)

5. Communities and people affected by crisis have access to safe and responsive mechanisms to handle complaints

Quality criterion: Complaints are welcomed and addressed

Use of community involvement in initial assessment, response identification (Chapter 4), process monitoring, and project reviews and evaluations provides opportunities for complaints to be heard (Chapter 8)

6. Communities and people affected by crisis receive coordinated and complementary assistance

Quality criterion: Humanitarian response is coordinated and complementary

Use of SEADS Principle 5 emphasizes coordinated responses within and across organizations

Use of minimum standards on systems-based assistance encourages coordination with multiple stakeholders (Minimum Standards 5.3, 6.3)

7. Communities and people affected by crisis can expect delivery of improved assistance as organizations learn from experience and reflection

Quality criterion: Humanitarian actors continuously learn and improve

Attainment of minimum standards is an iterative effort, with progressive improvements in assistance along the way

Use of SMART objectives (Minimum Standard 8.2), process monitoring (Minimum Standard 8.3), and impact evaluation of crop-related responses (Minimum Standard 8.5) contributes to learning

8. Communities and people affected by crisis receive the assistance they require from competent and well-managed staff and volunteers

Quality criterion: Staff are supported to do their job effectively and are treated fairly and equitably

Use of the minimum standards reinforces the importance of technical support and competencies required for crop-related crisis response. Minimum team competencies aligned with Annex B ensure competent staff participate in crop-related response design

9. Communities and people affected by crisis can expect that the organizations assisting them are managing resources effectively, efficiently, and ethically

Quality criterion: Resources are managed and used responsibly for their intended purpose

Use of decision trees provides a systematic process for considering all variables that could affect the use of project resources (Figures 5.1, 6.1, and 7.1)

Use of process monitoring supports financial accountability and real-time adjustments to project implementation (Minimum Standard 8.3)

Use of benefit-cost analysis supports measurement of livelihood impacts from crop-related responses (Minimum Standard 8.5)

Recommended reading

Details of references cited in this chapter are in Annex C. Further recommended reading includes:

Byrne, K. (2022). *Resources to strengthen adaptive management for livelihoods programming in emergency settings.* Mercy Corps (as part of the Strengthening Capacity in Agriculture, Livelihoods, and Environment (SCALE) Associate Award). https://www.fsnnetwork.org/resource/resources-strengthen-adaptive-management-livelihoods-programming-emergency-settings

Core Humanitarian Standard (CHS) Alliance (2020). *Humanitarian accountability report 2020: Are we making aid work better for people affected by crisis?* https://www.chsalliance.org/get-support/resource/har-2020/#:~:text=The%20 Humanitarian%20Accountability%20Report%202020%20is%20an%20evidence-based,five%20years%20after%20the%20launch%20of%20the%20CHS

Food and Agriculture Organization of the United Nations (FAO) (2017). *Yemen. Emergency livelihoods response plan: support to agriculture-based livelihoods in Yemen, January–December 2017.* FAO. http://www.fao.org/3/i6980e/i6980e.pdf

FAO & Feinstein International Center, Friedman School of Nutrition Science and Policy at Tufts University (2019). *Highlights on the resilience and vulnerability of populations affected by conflict.* Mind the Gap Briefing Paper 3. FAO & Tufts University. http://www.fao.org/3/ca7104en/CA7104EN.pdf

International Committee of the Red Cross (ICRC) (1977). *Protocol additional to the Geneva Conventions of 12 August 1949 and relating to the protection of victims of international armed conflicts (Protocol I), 8 June 1977,* Art. 54. https://ihl-databases .icrc.org/applic/ihl/ihl.nsf/INTRO/470?OpenDocument

Norwegian Refugee Council (2021). *Demystifying "tenure" for humanitarian practitioners.* https://www.globalprotectioncluster.org/wp-content/uploads/ Demystifying-Tenure-for-Humanitarian-Practitioners-2021.pdf

Office for the Coordination of Humanitarian Affairs (UNOCHA) (2020). *Global humanitarian response plan: COVID-19.* United Nations Coordinated Appeal April–December 2020, July update. UNOCHA. https://www.unocha.org/publication /global-humanitarian-response-plan/global-humanitarian-response-plan-covid-19-july-0

Torero, M. (2020, July 2). *Prepare food systems for a long-haul fight against COVID-19*. International Food Policy Research Institute. https://www.ifpri.org/blog/prepare-food-systems-long-haul-fight-against-covid-19

United Nations General Assembly (1948). *Universal declaration of human rights*, Art. 25(1). https://www.refworld.org/docid/3ae6b3712c.html

United Nations General Assembly (1989). *Convention on the rights of the child*, Art. 24. https://www.ohchr.org/en/professionalinterest/pages/crc.aspx

United Nations Office for Disaster Risk Reduction (2015). *Sendai framework for disaster risk reduction 2015–2030*. https://www.preventionweb.net/files/43291_sendaiframeworkfordrren.pdf

United Nations Office of the High Commissioner for Human Rights (2010). *The right to adequate food*. Human Rights Fact Sheet No.34. https://www.ohchr.org/Documents/Publications/FactSheet34en.pdf

World Bank (2020). *Poverty and shared prosperity 2020: Reversals of fortune*. https://openknowledge.worldbank.org/bitstream/handle/10986/34496/978146481624.pdf

World Bank (2021). *Labor force, total—Ethiopia*. https://data.worldbank.org/indicator/SL.TLF.TOTL.IN?locations=E

CHAPTER 3:
SEADS PRINCIPLES

> Annex A: Glossary contains definitions of various terms used in SEADS.

The five SEADS principles described in this chapter apply specifically to crop-related crisis response. They build on and complement the foundations described in Chapter 2: The Scope and Approach of SEADS, which apply in all humanitarian contexts. The five SEADS principles are:

1. Use livelihoods-based programming
2. Use a participatory approach in all aspects of crisis response
3. Commit to preparedness and early action
4. Consider climate change and minimize environmental impacts
5. Establish coordinated responses.

The principles are numbered to make cross-referencing easier; the numbers do not imply an order of importance or a sequence. They are all equally important.

SEADS Principle 1: Use livelihoods-based programming

Crop-related crisis responses should be based on livelihoods analysis and should aim to achieve one or more of the SEADS livelihood objectives.

Crop production sustains millions of smallholders, service providers, and markets around the world. The food they produce also helps sustain millions more. Crop producers affected by crisis may be unable to feed themselves or produce crops for sale.

Livelihoods-based programming emerged from the need to not only save lives, but also protect livelihoods in crisis response. Livelihoods programming also avoids undermining the local services, systems, and markets that enable recovery from crisis.

Livelihoods-based programming achieves one or more of the SEADS livelihood objectives (see Table 2.1). To meet those objectives, responses should:

- understand the direct and indirect role of crop production in livelihoods in the affected area
- support the systems, services, and markets that contributed to those livelihoods prior to the crisis
- coordinate with long-term development programs and policies.

The Sustainable Livelihoods Framework (Scoones 1998) is a useful tool for understanding livelihoods during normal (non-crisis) periods and to inform the SEADS response. When analyzing crop-based livelihoods, three factors are particularly important:

- access to land and water resources
- pre-crisis market characteristics
- seasonal conditions.

Access to land and water resources

All crop producers require safe and sustainable access to land and water resources. Without such access, crop-related crisis responses will have limited impact on livelihoods. Improving natural resource access can also improve preparedness and early recovery (Forcier Consulting Sudan 2017, Momoh & Browne 2019, ICRC 2019). In some crisis contexts, crop producers may already be dealing with land and water scarcity and degraded, depleted soils. Access to alternative natural resources is especially important for crop producers whose land or water has been contaminated with debris (boulders, uprooted trees, landslides) or unexploded ordnance and landmines, and for displaced people dependent on host communities for land and water resources.

Land tenure affects access to natural resources and therefore crop-related livelihoods. Livelihoods-based programming should consider land tenure and changes to access to land used for crop production. Where land access is hindered, crisis responses can include conflict management and clearing land of debris or unexploded ordnances to support crop production. NRC (2021) offers practical guidance and tools for considering tenure issues in crisis response. Land tenure for orphans can be an important issue to consider, especially in conflict/post-conflict settings.

Pre-crisis market characteristics

Livelihoods-based programming understands the market and considers the impact of technical options—market-based or in-kind delivery—on local crop-production value-chains. Where context allows, livelihoods-based programming favors market-based delivery over direct in-kind distribution.

Market-based delivery mechanisms are an increasingly common alternative to direct distribution in humanitarian response, as they provide increased flexibility and decrease response time. Market-based delivery mechanisms include all forms of conditional or unconditional cash and voucher assistance, such as digital or direct transfer mechanisms. While evidence of the livelihood impacts of market-based delivery mechanisms is not well documented (SEADS 2021), experience suggests that they support the sustainability and functionality of markets and delivery of diverse goods and services during and after the response. Market-based responses also help inject cash into local economies and support the livelihoods of local value-chain actors. Chapter 4: Initial Assessment for Crop-related Crisis Response provides guidance for ensuring market awareness in initial assessment and response identification.

Livelihoods-based programming recognizes the knowledge, skills, and experience of local service providers and their relationships along the value-chain and throughout the market system. Important value-chain actors include transporters, seed producers, extension agents, and input dealers. They can identify constraints to achieving livelihood objectives, and design and implement responses.

Livelihoods-based programming requires crop-related crisis response to be integrated into long-term development programs and policies, especially when preparing for or recovering from crisis. An important way of doing this is by working in support of local market systems, as these markets are usually critical to the longer-term livelihoods of crisis-affected people. Long-term development programs can also be a repository for market information that can serve to inform short-term crisis responses that support the same agricultural market systems. Flexible funds or "crisis modifiers" are an example of integrating crisis response into development. Integration avoids contradictions, increases livelihoods gains, and makes local crop production systems more resilient and sustainable.

Seasonal conditions

Crop production systems around the world are highly seasonal. Hence, the impact of a crisis on livelihoods depends on the timing, intensity, and duration of the crisis.

Livelihoods-based programs are tailored to the season and local agriculture calendar. Responses are timely; they are compatible with the current crop production stage and other seasonal variations, including seasonal labor and migratory patterns, household expenditure patterns, and health risks (see Minimum Standard 4.4) selecting response areas.

Livelihoods-based programming uses early-warning systems to develop informed, coordinated, and timely responses that reflect seasonal conditions. For example, after poor or failed rains, organizations should use meteorological forecasts to identify an appropriate crop-related crisis response. Where forecasts are for inadequate rainfall, organizations might postpone distributions to the following season and shift the focus to cash transfers for disaster risk reduction measures. Disaster risk reduction measures might include infiltration pits, contour ditches, terracing, and gully control, or in flood-affected areas the construction of berms or drainage canals to improve watershed management. Such measures help boost resilience and reduce longer-term risk to livelihoods.

SEADS Principle 2: Use a participatory approach in all aspects of crisis response

The affected population actively participates in the assessment, design, implementation, monitoring, and evaluation of the crop-related response.

Crop producers, input sellers, post-harvest processors, government extension agents, community-based organizations, NGO staff, financial service providers, wholesalers, and transporters have vast collective knowledge, skills, and experience of local crop production systems. They have a right to be recognized, respected, and heard. A participatory approach has two core elements:

- active engagement with affected crop producers, service providers, and market actors
- promotion of social equity.

Active engagement

Including different groups is central to the design, planning, and delivery of an effective crop-related crisis response and achieving the SEADS livelihood objectives. A participatory approach prioritizes active engagement through the different stages of the project cycle.

Initial assessment

Document local crop production systems, including the agriculture calendar, current and past cropping, level of mechanization, post-harvest processing, coping strategies, and pre-existing services and markets.

Design

Use information and analysis from the initial assessment to design a response that includes participatory approaches for targeting, planning, implementation, monitoring, and evaluation. Work with all relevant social groups.

Targeting

Involve the local administration and representatives of affected crop producers and marginalized groups in a community-based targeting approach in order to ensure appropriate allocation of inputs to all identified vulnerable groups.

Planning

Include the local administration, representative crop producers (both men and women), and any marginalized groups that will benefit from the response (see Chapter 4) in order to identify the most efficient and appropriate approach to participation.

Implementation

Deliver the implementation plan with community feedback, with built-in opportunities for review and adaptation.

Review during monitoring

Involve implementing partners, crop producers, and the local administration in reviewing participation levels and satisfaction, based on the understanding that adjustments may be needed throughout the project cycle to deliver a high-quality response.

Evaluation

After implementation of the response, evaluate the level of satisfaction and impact among all relevant social groups and by gender. Record how the response could have been done more efficiently (see Chapter 8: Impact-oriented Monitoring and Evaluation). Ensure stakeholder participation in the evaluation process.

In a participatory approach, implementing partners provide training and guidance through the life of the project and review progress and challenges regularly. In this way, the response will ensure respect for local actors, and use and consolidate local knowledge, skills, and experience. The participatory approach also recognizes and documents all local contributions made through focus groups, digital or in-person surveys, key informant interviews, and other in-kind contributions. Such documentation creates a partnership of equals with the different partners responsible for different inputs and deliverables.

Promotion of social equity

The rights-based foundations of crop-related crisis response promote social equity, without creating or reinforcing social inequality. A participatory approach analyzes and understands vulnerabilities and gives special attention to disadvantaged groups, such as children and orphans, women, the elderly, people living with disabilities, or groups marginalized because of factors such as religion, ethnicity, or caste. This analysis and understanding of their roles, rights, and responsibilities allow crop-related crisis responses to respond to different and specific household needs and abilities (see Chapter 4).

Responding to different and specific needs is important because different sociodemographic groups prioritize different crops and therefore may prefer different responses. Similarly, factors such as gender, culture, or different physical abilities may reduce some groups' input regarding what they grow and how they use the harvested crops. Initial assessment will identify the unique characteristics of a place and its people and will help to identify differences in people's engagement in crop production, service provision, and markets.

Participatory approaches ensure that people who are knowledgeable and sensitive about power dynamics help to design, implement, and evaluate responses. Equitable power dynamics is a characteristic of a well-functioning market, and appropriate community Participation in program design can help practitioners avoid reinforcing negative power dynamics among vendors. At a minimum, the design, planning, and implementation of a crop-related crisis response should recognize and ensure the Participation of:

- women and men of diverse ages, wealth, and social status, who are active in crop production, post-harvest processing, or marketing

- marginalized or vulnerable groups, including persons with disabilities, low castes, displaced people, and different ethnic groups or religions, who produce crops or who would benefit from producing food for themselves.

Gender is particularly important since women and men have different roles and responsibilities in crop production. In a crisis, they may also have access to different resources and hence different coping strategies that implementing partners must understand and recognize. In some cases, women's coping strategies may increase their vulnerability. For example, during and after conflict, if men and youth are away from home, women may take on new crop production tasks, including storage and sale, which may increase their exposure to abuse or exploitation. Documenting and adapting the response to reflect different gender roles and responsibilities will ensure adequate and appropriate support can be provided throughout the project cycle. Similar strategies and approaches are required for marginalized and vulnerable groups, also taking into account their specific rights.

A participatory approach should also be based on a sound understanding of crop producers' and service providers' access to the productive assets needed to support crop production. Displaced marginalized groups may be particularly vulnerable as they may not be recognized or welcomed by the larger displaced population, host community, or authorities. Indeed, they may be considered a threat to community stability, and there may therefore be considerable resistance to their participation in a crop-related crisis response.

SEADS Principle 3: Commit to preparedness and early action

Crop-related crises are anticipated, planned for, and responses resourced using the principles of disaster risk reduction and anticipatory action.

A commitment to preparedness in crop-related crisis response improves livelihood outcomes by identifying and prioritizing risks and taking action to manage them before they occur. Preparedness requires detailed knowledge of past crises. The participatory development of a historical timeline can provide this detailed knowledge and should include information on:

- peak hazard periods
- seasonal weather and conflict patterns
- seasonal production activities

- climate
- crop-based livelihood activities
- the historical occurrence and impact of the priority hazard(s)
- the availability of early-warning information to trigger anticipatory action.

Community-level preparedness planning should build capacity in local organizations, such as existing community institutions or dedicated emergency management bodies, so that these actors understand local risks and are able to reduce them. At the regional or country level, the humanitarian community may develop rapid response plans detailing specific crop-related response activities as part of preparedness planning.

Case Study 3.1 (see SEADS website) provides an example of an FAO rapid response and mitigation plan to avert humanitarian catastrophe in the Horn of Africa.

Organizations should review their administrative procedures to ensure that disaster risk reduction and anticipatory actions are administratively possible. For example, crop-related crisis responses may require the rapid procurement of large quantities of seed or tools, or debit cards, so contracts with transport companies, seed sellers, tool manufacturers, or financial service providers should be drafted in advance or, if possible, framework agreements should be set up that can be activated when a crisis occurs. Financial resources will need to be available and rapidly mobilized, particularly for anticipatory actions. Market-based approaches, including cash and voucher assistance, may result in increased flexibility and decreased response time.

Disaster risk reduction

Disaster risk reduction increases the ability of people affected by crisis to build back better after a crisis, increase their resilience, and withstand future shocks. Disaster risk prioritization identifies the risks to crop production that are most important to manage. It considers factors such as the frequency and seasonality of the risk, as well as which livelihoods, locations, and subsectors are most likely to be affected. Disaster risk prioritization should inform disaster risk reduction and preparedness planning. It is a pre-requisite for technically sound anticipatory action, which should be an integral part of disaster risk management systems. For anticipatory action to be effective, it should build on longer-term disaster risk reduction and preparedness efforts and be linked to response and recovery programming.

Disaster risk reduction in crop-related crisis responses might include initiatives such as developing and supporting early-warning systems that signal the likelihood of crop losses or damage from extreme weather events, or selecting crop varieties that are more difficult to steal or destroy, such as cassava.

Collaboration with longer-term development programs and national development priorities and policies is also part of disaster risk reduction, as the abrupt end of crisis funding can have negative consequences for communities affected by crisis. Coordination can inform strategies for phasing out or linking crisis responses to development responses. Local development actors can often contribute important knowledge, skills, and other resources in that regard. From a livelihood perspective, crisis responses in the recovery phase should converge with sustainable, long-term livelihood responses that are market aware.

Mainstreaming disaster risk reduction into development programs is increasing. It includes mapping the potential impact of future crises and setting aside funds for scaling up responses in case of a crisis. For example, in flood-prone crop production areas, locations for berms or drainage canals can be identified so they can be built or reinforced prior to the crisis occurring.

Anticipatory actions

Anticipatory actions are most often applied to a slow-onset crisis, such as one caused by drought, pests or diseases, and sometimes conflict-induced displacement. They are triggered by a forecast, combined with an analysis of the current situation, ahead of the peak of the expected impact. Examples of crop-related anticipatory actions include:

- facilitating access to drought-tolerant crop seeds between a drought forecast and the end of the planting period
- facilitating access to short-cycle crop seeds (such as vegetables and cowpeas) and small-scale water equipment between a drought forecast and the peak of a drought impact
- distributing sealable drums to store seeds and tools, or reinforcing crop-related infrastructure, between a cyclone or flood forecast and its occurrence
- supporting early harvest between a cyclone or flood forecast and its occurrence
- exploring ways to establish land access for populations likely to become displaced.

Early-warning systems and contingency plans are most effective when developed with local partners, with roles and responsibilities clearly defined and staff appropriately trained. Timely training on anticipatory action and contingency planning allows pre-planned responses to be rolled out more effectively, leading to a more positive impact on livelihoods (LEGS 2014, CARE 2017). Contingency planning may include pre-crisis assessments of possible alternative livelihoods for people at risk, particularly those whose livelihoods depend on slow-growing perennial crops. In anticipatory action and contingency planning, triggers for prompting action and the release of contingency funds must be specific, clearly defined, and pre-agreed. Linkages with early-warning systems are vital to support this process. Ideally, early-warning systems are based on readily and regularly available forecasts, seasonal observations, and information on current and projected vulnerability. A threshold should be associated with each piece of information monitored by the early-warning system, indicating a significant and actionable change in disaster likelihood and expected impact. In a complete anticipatory action system, surpassing an agreed number of thresholds should trigger the release of money for anticipatory action. Jones et al. (2020) outline seven guiding principles for selecting anticipatory actions. Chapter 4 provides details on selection of response areas, and timing tables (Tables 5.5, 5.6, 6.5, 6.6, 7.3, and 7.4) provide detail on which technical options would be appropriate.

SEADS Principle 4: Consider climate change and minimize environmental impacts

Crop-related crisis responses recognize the longer-term impacts of climate change in affected areas, and include measures that mitigate negative environmental impacts.

Climate change is driving an increase in the severity and frequency of natural disasters, which directly affect crop production. Key impacts of Climate change that affect crop producers include:

- changes to rainfall and temperature patterns, requiring changes to traditional crop preferences
- loss of biodiversity, including pollinating insects
- changes to crop growth patterns and nutrient load due to higher atmospheric carbon dioxide concentrations
- increases in pests, diseases, and invasive weeds.

Addressing such impacts in a way that supports achieving livelihood objectives requires climate-smart crop production responses. Such responses focus on climate change adaptation and mitigation through initiatives such as:

- integrated production systems, such as those that combine livestock and crop production

- energy-efficient production methods and infrastructure
- increased genetic diversity in crops and pollinators
- innovative water management
- crop selection based on soil assessment
- sustainable land rehabilitation
- consideration of alternative livelihoods.

The *Climate Smart Agriculture Sourcebook* (FAO 2022) provides comprehensive information and practical advice for ensuring that crop-related crisis responses consider climate change.

As well as climate change, environmental impact assessment and mitigation are important when designing any crop-related crisis response. Consider the direct impacts associated with natural resource use and the indirect impacts of associated activities, including procurement, transport, and training. There is an overwhelming evidence base that confirms the benefits of agro-ecological approaches to crop production. Team members trained and experienced in environmental science in crop-related crisis responses will therefore contribute to achieving the SEADS livelihood objectives and minimizing environmental impact.

Tools such as the Nexus Environmental Assessment Tool (NEAT+) (UNEP/OCHA Joint Environment Unit 2021) and the Green Recovery and Reconstruction Toolkit (WWF 2017) can also assist. They highlight the need to identify and mitigate environmental risks such as the potential for habitat destruction and water or soil contamination.

See also Commitment 3 and Commitment 9 of the *Core Humanitarian Standard* and Shelter and settlement standard 7: Environmental sustainability in the *Sphere Handbook*.

SEADS Principle 5: Establish coordinated responses

Crop-related crisis responses are coordinated, complementary, and do not interfere with activities that prioritize protection, food, shelter, water, and health inputs.

A coordinated response complements the delivery of protection, food, shelter, water, health, and other essential lifesaving humanitarian assistance in a crisis. This is especially important when required resources are limited, or the scale of a disaster is beyond the capacity of implementing partners to respond to all the identified needs. If resources are limited, the delivery of essential humanitarian assistance takes precedence over a crop-related crisis response.

However, once essential lifesaving assistance is routinely provided, crop-related crisis response should be coordinated and complementary. A coordinated response:

- aligns and complies with an agreed implementation strategy that is tailored to specific vulnerable sub-groups, minimizes duplication, identifies and addresses gaps, reduces environmental impact, and which local government has had an opportunity to endorse
- requires additional resources (time, human, financial) due to the increased complexity of the response, but pays off in more efficient implementation
- uses an agreed data collection approach that contributes to a database that is accessible to all actors (see Chapter 4 for more information about coordinating data collection and analysis)
- encourages shared technical expertise, leading to effective joint programming and shared use of resources and facilities
- provides a needs-based standardized level of support to crop producers across the affected area, reducing the need for affected crop producers to move between areas to secure different types of support from different actors in different locations
- promotes guidance on localization and cross-sectoral collaboration, and identifies roles, responsibilities, capacities, and interests of different stakeholders involved in the implementation.

In areas where development programs already support crop-related systems, services, and markets, it is essential for crop-related crisis responses to coordinate and harmonize with those existing programs. Likewise in a crisis-affected region, development programs should anticipate, plan for, and assign resources to crisis response.

A coordinated response requires more than harmonizing input packages, as the delivery of the same package across a wide area may overwhelm local markets. For example, if multiple organizations provide seed vouchers in a single market at the same time, seed price inflation may be triggered. This would reduce the benefit considerably for those who cash in vouchers later (see also SEADS Principle 1).

During a crisis, it is important to coordinate the response to achieve best use of resources. A coordinated response increases impact and resource efficiency. For example, providing or repairing irrigation equipment to support crop production should also consider livestock and human water needs. Similarly, cash support for seed purchases can be provided alongside a food ration (as seed protection) for the targeted populations, and it should be ensured that the targeted beneficiaries have the physical capacity for cultivation.

The local government in the area affected by a crisis is ultimately responsible for the overall planning and coordination of the response. However, if government capacity is limited, the government may opt to work in partnership with international humanitarian organizations, which can coordinate the response at national, sub-regional, and local levels. In this way, coordination extends from policy and strategy to effective local-level targeting and meeting specific local needs. Where the Global Food Security Cluster is activated, the Cluster can act in this coordination role.

To be effective, however, the coordinating mechanism needs access to adequate resources to address the many practical barriers to meaningful participation. These barriers include membership, language, logistics, and compliance issues associated with quality assurance, fiduciary risks, reporting requirements, and legal and policy barriers (including sanctions). Such issues challenge coordination, collaboration, and meaningful partnership between international and local actors. In some cases, it may be necessary to consider translation and interpretation services as a routine operational cost.

It may also be helpful to use digital communications tools, such as SMS, WhatsApp, Skype, and Facebook, to ensure that information about meeting locations, dates, times, and supporting documentation reaches all stakeholders. Meeting locations need to be safe and accessible for all implementing partners. Finally, it is important that barriers to coordination are periodically reviewed and the necessary adjustments made.

Recommended reading

Details of references cited in this chapter are in Annex C. Further recommended reading includes:

SEADS Principle 1: Use livelihoods-based programming

CALP Network (2011). *Glossary of terms.* https://www.calpnetwork.org/resources/glossary-of-terms/

FAO (2011). *Rabi 2010/11 agricultural intervention report: Part of FAO's flood response Pakistan.* FAO.

FAO (2012). *Voluntary guidelines on the responsible governance of tenure of land, fisheries and forests in the context of national food security.* https://www.fao.org/publications/card/en/c/I2801E/

Juillard, H., Mohiddin, L., Pechayre, M., Smith, G. & Lewin, R. (2017). *The influence of market support interventions on household food security.* Oxfam GB. https://policy-practice.oxfam.org/resources/the-influence-of-market-support-interventions-on-household-food-security-an-evi-620238/

Markets in Crises (2022). *Market based programming framework.* Catholic Relief Services (CRS). https://beamexchange.org/uploads/filer_public/28/ce/28ce6b54-c69c-481b-99c0-da7807ead5da/market_based_programming_framework_2022_compressed.pdf

Unger, E. & Chhatkuli, R. (2019). *Fit-for-purpose land administration in a post disaster context: Lessons and applications from Nepal.* UN-Habitat. https://seads-standards.org/wp-content/uploads/2021/04/Unger-and-Chhatkuli-2019.pdf

United Nations Human Settlements Programme (2010). *Land and natural disasters – guidance for practitioners.* UN-Habitat. https://unhabitat.org/sites/default/files/download-manager-files/Land%20and%20Natural%20Disasters%20Guidance%20for%20Practitioners.pdf

SEADS Principle 2: Use a participatory approach in all aspects of crisis response

ALNAP (2021). *Targeting for improved humanitarian response portal* [website]. UNHCR. https://targeting.alnap.org/

Catley, A., Burns, J., Abebe, D. & Suji, O. (2014). *Participatory impact assessment: A design guide*. Feinstein International Center, Friedman School of Nutrition Science and Policy at Tufts University. https://fic.tufts.edu/assets/PIA-guide_revised-2014-3.pdf

Geilfus, F. (2008). *80 Tools for participatory development: Appraisal, planning, follow-up and evaluation*. Inter-American Institute for Cooperation on Agriculture. https://www.betterevaluation.org/en/resources/guide/80_tools_for_participatory_development

Grand Bargain Localization Workstream (2020). *Guidance note on humanitarian financing for local actors*. Inter-Agency Standing Committeee (IASC). https://interagencystandingcommittee.org/system/files/2020-05/Guidance%20note%20on%20financing%20May%202020.pdf

International Institute for Environment and Development (IIED) (2021). *Participatory learning and action (PLA)*. IIED. https://www.iied.org/participatory-learning-action-pla

Walsh, S. & Sperling, L. (2019). *Review of practice and possibilities for market-led interventions in emergency seed security response*. A Feed the Future Global Supporting Seed Systems for Development Activity (S34D) report. United States Agency for International Development (USAID). https://doi.org/10.13140/RG.2.2.26610.32961

SEADS Principle 3: Commit to preparedness and early action

Mitchell, D., Myers, M. & Grant, D. (2014). Land valuation: a key tool for disaster risk management. *Land tenure journal 1*. FAO. https://eprints.leedsbeckett.ac.uk/id/eprint/5051/1/LandValuation_AKeyToolForDisasterRiskManagementPV-MYERS.pdf

Peters, K., Peters, L.E.R., Twigg, J. & Walch, C. (2019). *Disaster risk reduction strategies: Navigating conflict contexts*. Overseas Development Institute Working paper 555. https://cdn.odi.org/media/documents/12690.pdf

SEADS (2021). *Emergency agriculture interventions: Reviewing evidence on the impacts on livelihoods, food security, and nutrition*. https://seads-standards.org/wp-content/uploads/2021/04/SEADS_brief1_4.26.21.pdf

United Nations Office for Disaster Risk Reduction (2015). *Sendai framework for disaster risk reduction 2015–2030*. https://www.preventionweb.net/files/43291_sendaiframeworkfordrren.pdf

SEADS Principle 4: Consider climate change and minimize environmental impacts

EHA Connect (2022). *Food security, nutrition and livelihoods.* https://ehaconnect. org/clusters/food-security-nutrition-and-livelihoods/

FAO & World Health Organization (WHO) (2014). *The international code of conduct on pesticide management.* https://www.fao.org/fileadmin/templates/agphome/ documents/Pests_Pesticides/Code/CODE_2014Sep_ENG.pdf

FAO & World Bank (2018). *Rapid assessment of natural resources degradation in areas impacted by the refugee influx in Kakuma Camp, Kenya.* https://documents1. worldbank.org/curated/ru/526621571221184479/pdf/Rapid-Assessment-of-Natural-Resources-Degradation-in-Areas-Impacted-by-the-Refugee-Influx-in-Kakuma-Camp-Kenya.pdf

FAO & World Bank (2020). *Rapid assessment of natural resource degradation in refugee impacted areas in Northern Uganda.* 2nd edn. http://www.fao.org/ documents/card/en/c/CA7656EN

Global Affairs Canada (2018). *International humanitarian assistance – funding application guidelines for non-governmental organizations.* Government of Canada. https://www.international.gc.ca/world-monde/issues_development-enjeux_develo ppement/response_conflict-reponse_conflits/guidelines-lignes_directrices.aspx? lang=eng

Klenk, J. (2010). Green guide to construction. *In green recovery and reconstruction: Training toolkit for humanitarian aid (GRRT).* World Wildlife Fund & American Red Cross. https://files.worldwildlife.org/wwfcmsprod/files/Publication/file/6yv8ayzl1 y_Combined_GRRT.pdf?_ga=2.71116373.478864359.1636482104-1642110664. 1634207796

Norwegian Refugee Council (NRC) (2021). *Guidance note: HLP and natural resource due diligence in NRC.* https://www.globalprotectioncluster.org/wp-content/uploads /HLP-and-natural-resource-due-diligence-in-NRC-Guidance-Note-2021.pdf

Ochoa, K., Harrison, L., Lyon, N. & Nordentoft, M. (2019). *Looking through an environmental lens: Implications and opportunities for cash transfer programming in humanitarian response.* UNEP/OCHA Joint Environment Unit and the Global Shelter Cluster. https://reliefweb.int/attachments/159dd2aa-7bb9-3f48-b2a5-695048a1cd 2f/cashenvironment_-_implications_and_opportunities%20%281%29.pdf

Sphere (2019). *Reducing environmental impact in humanitarian response.* Thematic Sheet—Environment. https://spherestandards.org/wp-content/uploads/Sphere-thematic-sheet-environment-EN.pdf

UNEP/OCHA Joint Environment Unit (2017). *The environmental emergencies guidelines, 2nd edn.* Environmental Emergencies Centre. https://reliefweb.int/sites/reliefweb.int/files/resources/EE_guidelines_english.pdf

SEADS Principle 5: Establish coordinated responses

Global Food Security Cluster (2020). *2020–22 strategic plan.* World Food Programme. https://fscluster.org/sites/default/files/fsc_strategic_plan_20-22_signed_by_co_leads.pdf

World Bank (2016). *Who are the poor in the developing world?* Poverty and Shared Prosperity Report 2016: Taking on Inequality. Background Paper. https://documents1.worldbank.org/curated/en/187011475416542282/pdf/WPS7844.pdf

CHAPTER 4:
INITIAL ASSESSMENT FOR CROP-RELATED CRISIS RESPONSE

Minimum standards: initial assessment for crop-related crisis response

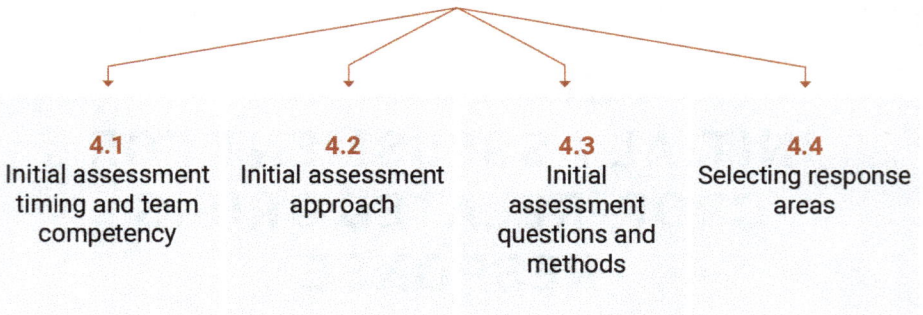

4.1
Initial assessment timing and team competency

4.2
Initial assessment approach

4.3
Initial assessment questions and methods

4.4
Selecting response areas

CHAPTER 4: INITIAL ASSESSMENT FOR CROP-RELATED CRISIS RESPONSE

> Annex A: Glossary contains definitions for some of the technical terms used in SEADS.

This chapter provides minimum standards for initial assessment and for deciding which response areas are relevant for a particular crisis situation. Using these minimum standards can help you determine:

- if a crop-related response is necessary, appropriate, and feasible
- which crop-related response type(s) is likely to have the most positive impact on livelihoods.

SEADS uses two levels of crop-related response:

- The **response area** is the general type of response, of which there are three types:
  - seed and seed systems (Chapter 5)
  - tools, equipment, and other non-seed inputs (Chapter 6)
  - crop-related infrastructure (Chapter 7).

This chapter focuses on the initial assessment of a crisis and the information and analysis that is needed to select one or more of these response areas. SEADS covers these three response areas in detail due to the evidence base and expert experience available for them.

- Within each response area are different **technical options**. The technical options provide specific guidance on different ways of designing and delivering crop-related assistance under each response area. Information on the technical options is provided in Chapters 5, 6, and 7. Decision trees in these chapters identify specific technical options that are most likely to have livelihood impacts within a given context.

Figure 4.1 shows how initial assessment relates to response area identification and the different resources SEADS provides for these activities.

Figure 4.1: Initial assessment determines if crop-related crisis response is necessary, appropriate, and feasible and informs response-area identification

1 Initial assessment

Initial assessment is timely and the assessment team is qualified and experienced
Minimum standard 4.1

Initial assessment is participatory and supported by secondary information
Minimum standard 4.2

Initial assessment is structured and uses appropriate participatory methods with communities and local actors
Minimum standard 4.3

Initial assessment is used to decide if a crop-related response is necessary, appropriate, and feasible.

2 Response-area identification

Response-area Identification Tool (RAIT) is used to maximize livelihood objectives
Minimum standard 4.4

Decision trees identify specific technical options
Chapter 5, Chapter 6, Chapter 7

Identified technical options can achieve livelihood objectives.

Note: If a crop-related response is not necessary, appropriate, or feasible, or will not have an impact on livelihoods, consider responses that are not crop related.

If initial assessment determines that a crop-related crisis response is necessary, appropriate, and feasible, organizations should identify the response areas that are likely to have the greatest positive impact on livelihoods (see Minimum Standard 4.4).

Although this chapter focuses on initial assessment and the selection of crop-related response areas, the information that is used for these activities is directly relevant to assessing accountability against the CHS (see Table 2.3 in Chapter 2: The Scope and Approach of SEADS) and the monitoring and evaluation of responses (see Chapter 8: Impact-oriented Monitoring and Evaluation).

The importance of initial assessment for crop-related crisis response

The livelihood impacts of crop-related responses are directly related to the quality of initial assessment and selection of the most appropriate response types. Due to the very wide variation in crisis contexts, and the role of crops in livelihoods, farming systems, and sociocultural environments, crop-related responses need to be tailored to specific communities and locations. Responses should be correctly timed relative to the crop production cycle in the crisis-affected area and take account of the cropping practices and preferences of vulnerable and marginalized groups. In contrast, responses that are based on weak assessment are more likely to cause harm or achieve low impacts.

Initial assessment can be the start of a participatory process that actively works with communities to analyze the crisis situation, leading to the joint selection of locally appropriate response types (see SEADS Principle 2: Use a participatory approach in all aspects of crisis response in Chapter 3: SEADS Principles). Further participatory analysis is then used to refine the response types based on the technical options in Chapters 5, 6, and 7.

Initial assessment and response-area identification minimum standards for crop-related crisis response

Minimum Standard 4.1: Initial assessment timing and team competency

Initial assessment is timely and the assessment team is qualified and experienced.

Key actions

- Initial assessment is timely relative to the need for immediate lifesaving humanitarian assistance (see Guidance note 1).

- The assessment team is competent in the use of participatory approaches and methods for the initial assessment of crop-related crisis responses (see Guidance note 2).

Guidance notes

1. **Assessment timing.** Activities related to crop-related crisis response should not interfere with or detract attention from lifesaving responses or basic needs. During a crisis, especially a rapid-onset crisis, the priorities in the immediate period after the event are often to save human lives and provide medical services, shelter, and other support. Critical resources such as transportation into affected areas can be limited at this time and need to be used to ensure that basic needs are met. The *Sphere Handbook* provides extensive guidance on assessing people's basic needs, and such assessments may be conducted by other organizations. Agencies and personnel involved in potential crop-related responses should time their initial assessments to take place after the basic needs of affected communities have begun to be met. In line with SEADS Principle 1: Use livelihoods-based programming the initial assessment should take into consideration the agriculture calendar and how information gathered may be different depending on when the assessment is completed. In line with SEADS Principle 5: Establish coordinated responses, the initial assessment of crop-related responses should be coordinated with other assessments to ensure timeliness and relevance. Joint assessment of crop and livestock issues is particularly relevant in areas with mixed farming systems or agro-pastoralism. Although this chapter focuses on initial assessment and the selection of response types, the selection of technical options and use of decision trees should follow on immediately and take place during the same visits to target populations.

2. **Team competency and composition.** Designing and conducting initial assessment requires specific knowledge and experience of participatory approaches and methods in emergency situations, and how to use participatory methods for the rapid assessment of crop-related issues. Designing and conducting initial assessment includes how to adapt participatory methods to specific contexts and how to cross-check information from participatory methods with secondary information during the assessment. Team members should have technical knowledge of local crop systems and be sufficiently experienced to probe the views of community members or informants such as local government officials. A competent assessment team should be diverse. It is important that assessment teams include men and women to gather perspectives from both

genders effectively. In cultures where it is inappropriate for men to meet directly with women or girls, the assessment team should hold separate meetings with men and women. Also see Annex B, SEADS Principle 2, and the *Core Humanitarian Standard Commitment 8*.

Minimum Standard 4.2: Initial assessment approach

Initial assessment is participatory and supported by secondary information.

Key actions

- Initial assessment is based on the active participation of crisis-affected communities and joint analysis of the crisis and its impacts (see Guidance note 1).
- Where possible, initial assessment is guided by pre-prepared emergency response plans and supported by pre-existing information (see Guidance notes 2 and 3).

Guidance notes

1. **Participation.** In line with SEADS Principle 2, crisis-affected communities should be actively involved in the initial assessment. A participatory approach means that information provided by community members is analyzed with them at the time of the assessment, leading to a common understanding of the impact of the crisis on livelihoods and whether a crop-related response is needed. When facilitated by experienced staff, the joint assessment can be the start of building trust and working relationships at community level, which is important for further analysis and decision making on response areas (this chapter) and specific technical options (Chapters 5, 6, and 7), as well as implementation and monitoring and evaluation (M&E) (Chapter 8). Weak participation during initial assessment increases the risk of agencies working with biased and inaccurate information, and this risk also applies to later stages of a response such as in response design and M&E. In crop-related crisis response there is a clear need for agencies to commit to

participatory approaches. For example, a survey in 2022 reported that only 64% of organizations active in crop-related response considered local and Indigenous knowledge to a large degree (Global Food Security Cluster, 2022).

2. Emergency response plans. In line with SEADS Principle 3: Commit to preparedness and early action agencies that implement development projects in crisis-prone areas should have emergency contingency plans in place. When these plans have been developed with communities and other local actors, the process of initial assessment can be more streamlined and rapid. Assuming that the type of emergency being assessed is the same as the emergency(ies) covered in the contingency plan, the initial assessment can focus on validating the plan and updating it with details of the actual emergency event and its impacts. Case Study 4.1 (see SEADS website) describes how preparedness can include the forecasting of potential disaster scenarios.

3. Pre-existing information. During a participatory assessment the validity of the findings partly depends on cross-checking with pre-existing secondary information. There are many different types of secondary information from different sources, and these will vary by context. It can include reports on: livelihoods; agriculture production and markets (including seasonality of production); food security and nutrition; previous crises and responses; sociocultural contexts; and roles of public and private sector actors in supporting crop production and markets. This information can be available in formal assessments conducted by governments, UN agencies or NGOs, consultants, or academic researchers, as well as in databases, geographic information systems, maps, and satellite images.Pre-crisis market assessments, using tools such as the Pre-Crisis Market Analysis Guidance (IRC 2016), may provide data on market prices and seasonal price fluctuations. The collection and analysis of pre-existing information can be time consuming but is often feasible during slow-onset and complex crises. In contrast, in areas prone to rapid-onset crises, the preferred use of this information is during the preparation of emergency contingency plans (Guidance note 2). To support the on-the-ground analysis of the crisis at community level and immediate cross-checking of information, the assessment team should be fully aware of pre-existing secondary information at the time of the assessment.

Minimum Standard 4.3: Initial assessment questions and methods

Initial assessment is structured and uses appropriate participatory methods with communities and local actors.

Key actions

- Initial assessment has a clear structure of key questions (see Guidance notes 1 and 2).
- Participatory methods are appropriate in relation to the key questions and sociocultural context (see Guidance note 3).
- Participants are selected to ensure that vulnerable groups are fully included in the analysis of crisis impacts and response preferences (see Guidance note 4).

Guidance notes

1. **Key questions—crisis impacts, livelihoods, and crops.** The key questions for the initial assessment are based on the need to understand the nature of the crisis, the impacts of the crisis on livelihoods in general, and the specific impact of the crisis on crop-related aspects of livelihoods. Notably, these specific crop-related impacts need to be considered in relation to the role of crops in livelihoods as a whole. This is because a crop-related response is more likely to be needed in areas where people rely heavily on crops for food or income, and where the crisis has caused major damage to crop systems or markets. In contrast, a crop-related response is less of a priority if crops play only a minor role in livelihoods, or if damage to crop systems and markets is not severe. Key questions will vary by context but can include:

- What is the type and severity of the crisis?
- What are the general impacts of the crisis on livelihoods?
- What are the specific impacts of the crisis on crop production systems, markets, and value-chain actors?
- In crisis-affected communities, how do these specific impacts vary by wealth, gender, or other types of vulnerability, and why?

- Is displacement of people a factor to consider, and is crop production important at the new location?
- What is the likelihood of a recurrence of the crisis?

See Appendix 4.1 for other example questions to determine if a crop-related response is necessary. These high-level questions can ensure a good understanding of the local crisis context and help agencies to decide if a crop-related response is needed. These include questions on the main crop production systems and management, the benefits of crop production (e.g., for consumption, income, or fodder), the roles of local service providers (value-chain actors), the role and performance of markets to crop-based livelihoods, and climate and natural disaster hazards and vulnerabilities. In mixed farming and agro-pastoral systems, the complementary roles of crops and livestock are important. Further details are provided in Appendix 4.1.

2.   **Key questions—operational context.** These questions will help you understand if a crop-related response is feasible relative to the operational context. Problems with physical access, insecurity, or other factors may mean that a response is not feasible, and therefore it should not be planned. Key questions on operational context can include:

- Can the crisis-affected population be physically accessed?
- What are the local security and protection issues related to communities, agency staff, and other actors such as service providers?
- Are effective and equitable communications and feedback systems in place and if not, can they be established?
- Is an effective coordination mechanism in place for humanitarian assistance and if not, what is the risk of duplicating efforts or inconsistent programming?
- Does the political and policy context enable an appropriate crop-related response?

See Appendix 4.1 for example questions to determine if a crop-related response is feasible. Also review SEADS Principle 5 as you prepare to answer these questions. Some of these questions may need to be revisited depending on the response area or technical options under consideration. For example, some types of response, such as cash transfers, can raise specific security risks.

3.   **Assessment methods selection.** Participatory methods should be used to gather and analyze information at community level. Information can be gathered using interviews with key informants, a review of security or other reports, and by referring to other types of secondary information. To ensure a systematic approach

to the assessment, it is useful to make a table outlining the key questions along with the method(s) to be used for each question and the people who will be involved for each question. At community level a wide range of Participatory methods are available for answering questions on topics such as the relative importance of different livelihood activities, relative sources of food and income, the seasonality of crop production and market prices, access to markets and sellers, and the roles and preferences for different types of crop-related support. Guidelines for using Participatory methods for crop systems are available (e.g., Stewart 1998; Schoonmaker Freudenberger 2008) but these methods should be selected specifically to answer key questions and adapted according to local contexts. The ability to select and adapt Participatory methods is an important aspect of team competency (Minimum Standard 4.1). Across all participatory methods, semi-structured interviews (SSIs) are used either to support other methods or as a stand-alone method.

Typically, initial assessments use a mix of qualitative information and information on quantities, prices, and other numerical data. Participatory methods such as SSIs can produce not only qualitative descriptions, but also absolute figures such as crop yields, market prices, and distances to services or markets. Similarly, Participatory maps can be used to estimate actual areas of land under cultivation by crop type or areas of land that is damaged or inaccessible. Proportional methods are useful for understanding the relative importance of an item compared to other items, for example, the annual proportion of total household income derived from crops relative to other sources of income.

4. Participants. An important aspect of the initial assessment is to ensure that vulnerable groups are fully included in the process. This means that these groups have to be identified. Often separate meetings and focus groups should be organized for these groups. At least three specific groups are relevant to crop-related responses: vulnerable women (or female-headed households), poorer crop producers in a given area, and groups who are marginalized through age, disability, ethnicity, or religion. The roles of crops in the livelihoods of these groups, their selection and management of crops, their decision making, and their preferred types of support need to be understood to ensure that responses are relevant and timely for them. Relevant participatory methods should be repeated with selected vulnerable groups and the findings compared to the general community. In addition to working with community members during the initial assessment, a wide range of other people can provide valuable information. These people may be: local government workers, including market officials and agricultural extension workers; traders, transporters, and input suppliers; and staff from development agencies and programs. The involvement of these participants is important for cross-checking and validating information gathered using participatory methods and, in some cases, can include informal assessment of their capacity and potential roles in a crop-related response. As described under SEADS Principle 1 supporting local services and markets is a key element of supporting livelihoods.

Minimum Standard 4.4: Selecting response areas

A systematic approach is used to select response areas and maximize livelihood impacts.

Key actions

- Conduct further rapid analysis to fill key information gaps related to the selection of response areas (see Guidance note 1).
- Select targeting criteria and methods (see Guidance note 2).
- Review and understand SEADS livelihood objectives and their relevance to your context (see Guidance note 3).
- Use the response-area identification tool (RAIT) to identify potential response areas (see Guidance notes 4, 5, 6, 7, 8).
- Use the decision trees in the appropriate technical chapters to identify specific technical options and related minimum standards to meet (see Guidance note 9).

Guidance notes

1.   **Information gaps.** If the initial assessment concludes that a crop-related response is needed and feasible, further information may be needed to support the selection of a response area. In particular, this selection should be guided by the potential livelihood impacts of responses, and the aim of maximizing impacts within a given context and for specific target groups. In addition, livelihoods-based responses should aim to work with local service providers, input suppliers, and market systems where possible. Further information may be needed on the availability and capacity of these actors and systems to guide the selection of response areas.

Further information gaps will vary widely according to context but could include further analysis of social norms and the roles that different household members play in various aspects of crop production, particularly related to gender and age. See Appendix 4.1 for example questions to determine how sociocultural factors will influence livelihood impacts from a crop-related response. See SEADS Principle 2 for important issues related to the socio-cultural context and protecting vulnerable groups. Case Study 4.2 (see SEADS website) shows how sociocultural information played a role in identifying activities in a project in South Sudan.

If the livelihood system in your context is agro-pastoral or mixed farming, information will be needed on specific livestock components and crop–livestock interactions (for example, the use of crop residues as fodder and the use of manure as fertilizer). Chapter 3 of LEGS provides support for understanding the role of livestock in a community.

2.   **Targeting criteria and methods.** The process of selecting response areas will be influenced by the types of crop producer who are most in need of assistance. These producers will be identified during the initial assessment (Minimum Standard 4.3) but further contact with communities may be needed to ensure that relevant and appropriate targeting criteria are developed. Commonly used criteria for crop-related responses, such as "limited access to land" or "poor road or market infrastructure," have different meanings across different regions and sociocultural contexts. Clear definitions help avoid inclusion and exclusion errors. Review the four Protection Principles in the *Sphere Handbook* for important considerations when developing and defining targeting criteria.

Community participation is also needed to support the transparent and impartial selection of participants, based on the agreed targeting criteria (see SEADS Principle 2). Targeting methods may include blanket targeting (covering the whole community), targeting of a specific category (such as gender, age, or geographical area), and self-selection. Once targeting criteria and the process for selecting participants are agreed by the organization and the community, the affected communities should control the targeting process as much as possible to avoid concerns about inequitable distribution of benefits. Check targeting during project implementation to ensure that vulnerable groups continue to be prioritized and not put at risk (see the Protection Principles in the *Sphere Handbook*). ALNAP (2021) provides additional information and tools for targeting. The questions in all the topics presented in Appendix 4.1 will help you better understand who you need to target.

3.   **Relevance of SEADS livelihood objectives**. Different response areas can be used, either alone or in combination, to achieve one or more of the SEADS livelihood objectives (see Chapter 2). Given the context, each livelihood objective may or may not be relevant. Using the findings of the initial assessment (Minimum Standards 4.2 and 4.3), you can consider and understand the relevance of each objective to your context. Targeted participants may need provision of immediate livelihood benefits (Objective 1); protection of their livelihoods (Objective 2); rebuilding or support for production, infrastructure, and systems to ensure continuity of their livelihoods (Objective 3); or a combination of multiple objectives. Appendix 4.4 links each response area to one or more of the SEADS livelihood objectives. It also suggests a minimum project duration for each.

4.   **Systematic response identification**. A systematic decision-making approach to identifying response areas strengthens the quality, relevance, and impact of a crop-related response. The SEADS RAIT will help you identify which potential response areas will have the greatest livelihood impact. The RAIT is a participatory tool that uses a matrix to show multiple response areas and their potential impact on livelihoods. Once the matrix is completed, the RAIT shows the relevant impact of each response area, including responses with no expected impact. You can then select which response areas to explore further in Chapters 5, 6, and 7. This systematic response identification tool supports strategic decision making before a specific technical option is selected (see Guidance note 9); it precedes decisions on issues such as the modality of delivering assistance. It also avoids repeating responses in situations and contexts where the response is not relevant or timely. A completed RAIT can be provided to donors to justify why your proposal focuses on a certain response area or why you may have rejected other areas. The RAIT is based on the participatory response identification matrix (PRIM) that has been used with success since 2009 by the LEGS livestock community. Considering livelihood objectives early in the design process can move organizations where necessary, beyond "business as usual." Appendix 4.2 features a completed RAIT, along with an explanation of the process that was used to complete it. A RAIT template, which you can use as the basis of your own RAIT, is in Appendix 4.3.

5.   **Information needed to use the RAIT**. To use the RAIT, you need the initial assessment findings (Minimum Standards 4.2 and 4.3) and a basic understanding of project design and implementation timelines for the three SEADS response areas:

- seed and seed systems (Chapter 5)
- tools, equipment, and other non-seed inputs (Chapter 6)
- crop-related infrastructure (Chapter 7).

You will also need to understand your implementation team's competencies (see Annex B). Chapters 5, 6, and 7 provide further detail on each of the three response areas and the minimum standards for various technical options in each.

6.   **Participatory approach to response identification.** The RAIT should be used with groups of stakeholders, including people from the affected communities and other people such as local service providers and key informants (local community, local and national authorities, civil society and private sector stakeholders, and other humanitarian actors). Be sure to include representatives of vulnerable groups and take into consideration gender and age aspects. A participatory approach as described in SEADS Principle 2 can be used in each step of completing the RAIT.

7.   **Timing of the RAIT.** The RAIT should be done as part of the initial assessment and planning for a crop-related crisis response. It can also be done before a crisis as part of your preparedness planning or when designing organizational agriculture and/or food security strategies. Doing the RAIT outside of a crisis allows your organization to identify response areas that are likely to have a significant impact on livelihoods in your operational context (see SEADS Principle 3).

8.   **Completing the RAIT.** There are three steps to completing the RAIT:

Step 1: Identify relevant crop production stages for each response area. A relevant stage is one that occurs during the time in which the response will be implemented. Understanding how the crop production cycle aligns with the potential project cycle is critical to determining this relevance. Stakeholders can help interpret initial assessment findings to determine this relevance. The following questions can be asked of the group to determine relevant stages: What stage of the crop production cycle will we be in when the response starts? How long will it take us to deliver the assistance to the affected communities? What stage will we be in then? For those stages that are not relevant, mark the corresponding cell with N/A (for "not applicable").

Step 2: Rate each response area for its potential impact on each livelihood objective. Moving across each row to each relevant cell (i.e., those not marked with N/A), determine the level of impact that can likely be achieved. When a response could have a "significant impact" mark a 3 in the cell. When a response could have "some impact" mark a 2 in the cell. When a response could have "little impact" mark a 1 in the cell. When a response is not likely to have any impact, mark N/A in the cell. When you have finished one row, move to the next, until all cells have been filled.

Step 3: Prioritize the response area(s). Looking across all combinations, identify those with the highest scores. Response areas with the highest scores have the greatest potential for impact on livelihoods, are most feasible, and are within your organization's capabilities to execute. For example, in the RAIT scenario in Appendix 4.2 the seed and seed systems response area is likely to have a significant impact on protecting essential crop-related livelihoods. A RAIT template is available in Appendix 4.3.

9.   Decision trees. Do not explore response areas with little or no potential for livelihood impact (score of 1 or N/A). However, once you have identified the highest-rated response areas, go to the chapter that corresponds to that response area (Chapter 5, 6, or 7). Review the importance of the response area, the technical options, and the timing tables as set out in those chapters. Use initial assessment findings to complete the decision trees in those chapters to identify one or more technical options, then work through all of the minimum standards that apply to your context. The decision tree may indicate you should not undertake activities in the response area(s). In this case, seek additional information to complete the decision tree or return to the RAIT and consider different response areas with high potential for livelihood impact.

Recommended reading

Details of references cited in this chapter are in Annex C. Further recommended reading includes:

Byrne, K. (2022). *Applying adaptive management to livelihoods in emergency settings: challenges and opportunities.* Mercy Corps (as part of the Strengthening Capacity in Agriculture, Livelihoods, and Environment (SCALE) Associate Award). https://www.fsnnetwork.org/resource/applying-adaptive-management-livelihoods-emergency-settings-challenges-and-opportunities

Byrne, K. (2022). *Resources to strengthen adaptive management for livelihoods programming in emergency settings.* Mercy Corps (as part of the Strengthening Capacity in Agriculture, Livelihoods, and Environment (SCALE) Associate Award). https://www.fsnnetwork.org/resource/resources-strengthen-adaptive-management-livelihoods-programming-emergency-settings

CHS Alliance (2014). *Core humanitarian standard on quality and accountability.* https://corehumanitarianstandard.org/the-standard/language-versions

Cosgrave, J., Buchanan-Smith, M. & Warner, A. (2016). *Evaluation of humanitarian action (EHA) guide.* ALNAP. https://www.alnap.org/help-library/evaluation-of-humanitarian-action-guide

Food and Agriculture Organization of the United Nations (FAO) (2019). *The programme clinic. Designing conflict-sensitive interventions: Approaches to working in fragile and conflict-affected contexts. Facilitation guide.* https://www.fao.org/resilience/resources/resources-detail/en/c/1206211/

FAO & International Labour Organization (2009). *The livelihood assessment tool-kit: Analysing and responding to the impact of disasters on the livelihoods of people.* https://www.fao.org/resilience/resources/resources-detail/en/c/171069/

International Federation of Red Cross and Red Crescent Societies (2013). *Baseline basics.* https://www.betterevaluation.org/sites/default/files/Baseline%20Basics%202013.pdf

Lorenzen, H. & Sullivan, L. (2021). *Sphere in context and for assessment, monitoring, evaluation and learning.* Sphere. https://www.spherestandards.org/resources/sphere-in-context-and-for-assessment-monitoring-evaluation-and-learning/

OECD/DAC Network on Development Evaluation (2019). *Better criteria for better evaluation: Revised evaluation criteria, definitions and principles for use.* https://www.oecd.org/dac/evaluation/revised-evaluation-criteria-dec-2019.pdf

SEADS (2021). *Emergency agriculture interventions: Reviewing evidence on the impacts on livelihoods, food security and nutrition.* https://seads-standards.org/wp-content/uploads/2021/04/SEADS_brief1_4.26.21.pdf

Appendix 4.1: Example questions to gather initial and technical data

The following are suggested questions to help you gather information described in Minimum Standards 4.2 and 4.3. These questions can be adapted to your context.

Is a crop-related response appropriate?

These questions will help you gather data on the role of crop production and markets in livelihoods (see Guidance note 1 of Minimum Standard 4.3).

1. Do crops play a significant role in the livelihoods of the affected people and is a crop-related response therefore appropriate? If so, is a market-based response also appropriate?
2. What are the main livelihood strategies in the affected area in normal times? Is the target population interested in engaging in crop production?
3. What crops and which varieties are grown, what area is cultivated of each, what quantities are harvested, and what are the key uses of crops (for food, fodder, or seed, or to barter, pay debts, or sell)?
4. What is the relative importance of different crops as staple foods? What is the seasonality of consumption of those foods?
5. What percentage of household income is derived from crop production in normal times?
6. What are the features of the agriculture calendar? How many cropping cycles are possible in one year? Which crops are produced in each cycle? What is their relative importance to household food security and income?
7. What are the main coping strategies and indicators for difficult times (for example, less frequent or less preferred meals, changes in crop choice, changes in market sales, dispersal of household members, sale of assets)?
   a. Do these strategies have negative implications for future crop-based activities?

b. What are the possible acute and chronic drivers of these strategies (for example, environmental, climate, weather, economic, social, political)?

8. Is production primarily intensive (in close quarters, limited space, close to home) or extensive (spread out, potentially far from home)?
9. What are the key shocks or crises impacting household food security and livelihoods (for example, climate change, conflict, health)?

a. How do these shocks affect crop production and population displacement?
b. Which environmental hazards pose a threat to future crop production or may cause displacement?

10. What services and facilities are usually available?
11. Which markets do crop producers use to buy inputs and sell products? How far are they, and can all people access these markets in normal times?
12. What relationships exist along the crop value-chain; for example, between formal and informal input sellers, market management committees, transporters, producers, producer-processors, end markets, and policy makers?
13. What are common challenges for people selling inputs and crop products in these markets in normal times?
14. What are common challenges for buyers trying to access these products?
15. Are essential crop production inputs (goods and services) generally available, affordable, and of suitable quality in normal times?

Is a crop-related response necessary?

These questions will help you gather data on the crisis context (see Guidance note 1 of Minimum Standard 4.3).

1. Is an emergency intervention necessary?
2. Is it a rapid-onset, slow-onset, or complex crisis?
3. What is the cause of the crisis (for example, drought, flood, conflict)?
4. Which phase has the crisis reached (immediate aftermath, early recovery, recovery)?
5. What populations and geographic zones or regions are affected?
6. What has been the impact of the crisis on crop production strategies? Specifically:

a. At what point in the agriculture season did the crisis occur (for example, planting, harvest)?
b. What is the impact on access to fields, orchards, or garden plots?
c. What is the impact on access to water resources for irrigation?
d. What is the impact on transportation of people and goods to and from fields, orchards, or garden plots?

    e. What is the impact on the labor force used for field preparation, planting, weeding, harvesting, and processing?

    f. What is the impact on services and facilities that are usually available (such as government administration and extension, seed multiplication and certification, private sector technical assistance, or financial services)?

    g. What is the impact of the crisis on natural resources?

    h. What is the impact of the crisis on the division of labor by gender and age?

    i. What is the impact on crop-related markets for inputs and sales?

    j. What plans do the affected people have for future crop production?

7. What is the impact of the crisis on annual, perennial, and horticulture crops? Specifically:

    a. Have crops been lost? If so, how significant are the losses?

    b. Have perennial crops been damaged? If so, how significant is the damage?

    c. Has there been an impact on production assets (such as equipment, machinery, or storage)? If so, how significant is the impact?

8. What is the forecast (where relevant) for the coming season (such as anticipated drought, floods, increasing insecurity, or access to food)?

9. How has the crisis affected the population and specific vulnerable groups?

    a. Who has been most impacted by the disaster? Consider age, gender, wealth, ethnic, or other groups. How have these populations been affected?

    b. Do households have continued access to adequate and healthy food?

    c. What are current food security levels?

    d. Can vulnerable groups continue with crop-related livelihood activities?

10. Has there been significant migration or displacement of all or parts of the affected populations?

    a. If so, who has migrated and do they still have access to their fields, orchards, or garden plots?

    b. What is the impact on the host community?

Is a crop-related response feasible?

These questions will help you gather data on the operational context (see Guidance note 2 of Minimum Standard 4.3).

1. What is the operating environment?

2. What are potential logistical constraints and areas of overlap or potential complementarity with other stakeholders?

3. Who are the key humanitarian actors in the affected area, what are they doing, or what are they likely to do?

4. Is any stakeholder playing a coordination role?
5. What is the history of crisis response in the affected area, both positive and negative, and what are the lessons learned from it?
6. What is the current operational context? The following questions (a through f) become especially significant, and in some cases identify insurmountable barriers to implementing a response, in conflict situations:

   a. How are communications functioning?
   b. What is the security situation?
   c. What are the implications for movement to and from fields, orchards, and garden plots?
   d. What are the key protection issues facing crop producers?
   e. What is the condition of the current infrastructure, such as roads and transport?
   f. Are there any cross-border crop-related issues or threats (such as locusts, fall armyworm)?

7. In situations of conflict, what are the causes and the implications for programming?
8. What political factors and timelines have the potential to affect programming?
9. What is the context for supporting or hindering crop-related activities?

   a. Have there been recent, or recurrent, efforts to support crop-related livelihood activities?
   b. Are there risks that goods provided by crop-related crisis response could be reallocated to another use (for example, fertilizer for explosives or hand tools as weapons)?
   c. What policy and/or legal constraints affect crop production? Examples include seed certification requirements, bans on genetically modified seed, restricted or prohibited pesticide use, security of tenure, coordination of aid organizations, national emergency management policies, and organizational policies of key stakeholders.
   d. Have recent changes in policy affected vulnerability?

10. What are the capacity and constraints of the market system in the target area? Pre-Crisis Market Analysis guidance (IRC 2016) and the *EMMA Toolkit* (Albu 2010) include detailed market assessment processes and key questions.
11. How have supply chains for critical inputs and services been impacted?

    a. In what way has the number or types of sellers in these markets changed as a result of the crisis?
    b. Has the availability or quality of essential crop-related inputs, goods, and services changed since the crisis? Are sellers still able to buy, store, and sell sufficient quality and quantities of inputs and services? (See Appendix 5.1: Initial assessment checklist for seed and seed systems responses,

Appendix 6.1: Initial assessment checklists for tools, equipment, and other non-seed input responses, and Appendix 7.1: Initial assessment checklist for crop-related infrastructure responses.)

c. Are sellers able to increase their stocks if needed to respond to increased demand from a market-based response?

d. Are financial services still available?

12. Since the crisis, can people from all ethnic, religious, political, and social groups access key markets? If not, what challenges do affected people face to access markets?

13. How have prices of crop-related inputs, goods, services, and products increased or decreased in these markets since the crisis and how do these changes impact affected people?

14. Since the crisis, are there any tensions related to ethnic, religious, political, or social affiliations in these markets?

15. How do people prefer to receive assistance (cash, voucher, in kind, other)?

What sociocultural factors influence the possibility and likelihood of livelihood impacts from a crop-related response?

These questions will help you gather data on the sociocultural context (see Guidance note 1 of Minimum Standard 4.4).

1. What is the role of non-crop-related livelihoods in the area?

2. What are the different social and wealth groups in the area?

3. How does wealth status affect crop production and use of crops?

4. What specific social inequities exist in the affected area?

5. How do social norms influence which groups of people produce perennial, annual, or horticulture crops, with particular reference to wealth and vulnerability?

6. What roles do different household members play in crop production, and how do gender and age affect that? Do those roles vary across agriculture seasons?

7. What responsibilities do different household members have for making decisions related to household food consumption, crop production and sales, and the use of income derived from crop sales?

8. What key social relationships and power dynamics affect crop production?

9. How do family customs or traditional knowledge influence how crops are used and how household income is managed? Who controls the use of crops?

10. What Indigenous knowledge informs the way crop producers interact with each other to produce, store, or market crops?

11. What customary institutions and leaders are involved in crop production, and what are their roles?

12. How do family customs or traditional knowledge help people cope with a crisis and adapt to new livelihood contexts?
13. What common terms or concepts in local languages describe people's relationship to crop production?
14. Do differences in culture, power relationships, livelihood groups, and/or age groups lead to misunderstanding, tension, or competition over resources necessary for crop production?

How well are local services, input suppliers, and markets functioning?

These questions will help you identify the local actors and how the crisis has affected their abilities (see Guidance note 1 of Minimum Standard 4.4).

1. Are local actors with technical skills still in the affected area?
2. Are these actors still able to support the affected community?
3. Are any government employees with crop-production skills or infrastructure knowledge part of the community affected by a crisis?
4. Are any value-chain actors with expertise in crop production part of the community affected by a crisis?
5. What essential crop-production services did these actors provide prior to the crisis?
6. What resources do local technicians have to do their jobs?
7. What resources are they lacking?

What are appropriate targeting criteria and methods?

These questions will help you establish the targeting criteria and methods to determine the most vulnerable groups to be assisted (see Guidance note 2 of Minimum Standard 4.4).

1. How do social and wealth groups differ among themselves regarding: access to land, quality of land, crops cultivated, area under cultivation, means/assets available for cultivation, use of inputs and labor, level of self-sufficiency, income sources, distribution of expenditures, level of food security, ability to sell crops, and ability to recover by themselves?
2. Which social and wealth groups are more vulnerable or affected by the crisis than others?
3. Are there existing safety net groups in the community, and what are their characteristics and capacities?

4. Which groups/people in the community are recognized or trusted by everybody in the village? Who are the "power players" in the community?

Appendix 4.2: RAIT example

This example shows how participants in a facilitated workshop used the RAIT to determine priority response areas for a rapid-onset crisis caused by heavy rain and floods in Gaza. The participants used data gathered during the initial assessment. In this scenario, participants were all staff of a humanitarian organization and one key informant they were able to bring into the discussion by phone. They knew that:

- A significant amount of field crops and vegetables were destroyed during three weeks of heavy rain and floods.
- Irrigation systems were flooded; silt had built up in the channels and irrigation equipment (pumps, gates) was damaged.
- Funds were available to respond immediately.
- The sowing season had passed for the current cropping season.
- Before the crisis, crop production provided more than 50% of household income in the area.
- To make up for the certain lack of income due to the missed sowing season, conditional cash was needed to buy inputs before the next season.
- Locally tested flood-tolerant seed varieties were available and preferred by participants, but were not widely used. The high cost of flood-tolerant seed varieties was considered in the calculations of cash assistance to encourage use.
- Irrigation channels could be cleared using a cash-for-work scheme before the next planting season. This would prepare the infrastructure for next season's production and increase its ability to withstand future floods, while also allowing households to earn cash.
- Private contractors were available to repair and extend the lifespan of equipment and storage facilities before the next season.

The workshop facilitator led the participants through the three-step process to complete the RAIT (see Guidance note 8 of Minimum Standard 4.4). Figure A4.1 shows the completed RAIT.

Crucial aspects of the workshop discussion are described in the following steps. In this scenario, the next step would be to understand the seed and seed system response area (Chapter 5), its technical options and timing, and then complete the decision tree. The discussion informed the selection of priority response areas and could also inform selection of technical options.

Figure A4.1: An example of a completed response-area identification tool (RAIT)

LIVELIHOOD OBJECTIVES BY RESPONSE AREA	STAGE OF THE CROP PRODUCTION CYCLE DURING WHICH THE RESPONSE WILL OCCUR			
	Pre-production planning (for example, crop or seed selection)	Production (for example, land preparation, crop management)	Post-production (for example, harvesting, storage, processing)	Marketing (for example, market access, transport)
Seed and seed systems (Chapter 5)				
SEADS livelihood objective 1: Provide immediate livelihood benefits	1	n/a	n/a	n/a
SEADS livelihood objective 2: Protect essential crop-related livelihoods	3	n/a	n/a	n/a
SEADS livelihood objective 3: Rebuild or support crop-related production, infrastructure, and systems to strengthen livelihoods	2	n/a	n/a	n/a
Tools, equipment, and other non-seed inputs (Chapter 6)				
SEADS livelihood objective 1: Provide immediate livelihood benefits	n/a	n/a	n/a	n/a
SEADS livelihood objective 2: Protect essential crop-related livelihoods	n/a	n/a	n/a	n/a
SEADS livelihood objective 3: Rebuild or support crop-related production, infrastructure, and systems to strengthen livelihoods	n/a	n/a	n/a	n/a
Crop-related infrastructure (Chapter 7)				
SEADS livelihood objective 1: Provide immediate livelihood benefits	3	n/a	n/a	n/a
SEADS livelihood objective 2: Protect essential crop-related livelihoods	n/a	3	2	n/a
SEADS livelihood objective 3: Rebuild or support crop-related production, infrastructure, and systems to strengthen livelihoods	n/a	3	n/a	n/a

Legend for scoring			
3 Significant impact on livelihood objective	**2** Small impact on objective	**1** Very little impact on objective	**n/a** No impact on livelihood objective OR crop production stage is not applicable for your response

Step 1: Identify relevant crop production stages for each response area.

- Because the crops were completely destroyed, the participants agreed that nothing should be done related to marketing. They marked all the cells below marketing with "n/a".
- The participants agreed that there could be appropriate responses for the pre-production/planning, production, and post-production stages, so they left those cells blank.

Step 2: Rate each response area for its potential impact on each livelihood objective.

- The participants worked through the matrix, starting with pre-production/planning and working down through production and finally post-production. The questions, answers, and responses recorded in the RAIT for the pre-production/planning column were:
  - Question: "What is the potential impact of seed and seed systems response on providing immediate livelihood benefits during pre-production/planning?"
    Answer: Little impact
    Matrix response: They marked a 1 in the appropriate cell.
  - Question: "What is the potential impact of a seed and seed systems response on protecting essential crop-related livelihoods during pre-production/planning?"
    Answer: Significant impact
    Matrix response: They marked a 3 in the appropriate cell.
  - Question: "What is the potential impact of a seed and seed systems response on rebuilding or supporting crop-related production, infrastructure, and systems to strengthen livelihoods during pre-production/planning?"
    Answer: Some impact
    Matrix response: They marked a 2 in the appropriate cell.
  - Question: "What is the potential impact of a tools, equipment, or other non-seed inputs response on providing immediate livelihood benefits during pre-production/planning?"
    Answer: No impact. A tools, equipment, or other non-seed inputs response is not appropriate as there is no damage to these items.
    Matrix response: They marked n/a in all cells related to tools, equipment, and other non-seed responses because a response in this area is not necessary.

- Question: "What is the potential impact of a crop-related infrastructure response on providing immediate livelihood benefits during pre-production/planning?"
  Answer: Significant impact
  Matrix response: They marked a 3 in the appropriate cell.
- Question: "What is the potential impact of a crop-related infrastructure response on protecting essential crop-related livelihoods during pre-production/planning?"
  Answer: No impact
  Matrix response: They marked n/a in the appropriate cell.
- Question: "What is the potential impact of a crop-related infrastructure response on rebuilding or supporting crop-related production, infrastructure, and systems to strengthen livelihoods during pre-production/planning?"
  Answer: No impact
  Matrix response: They marked n/a in the appropriate cell.

Step 3: Prioritize the response area(s) that have the greatest potential for impact on livelihoods (those with the highest scores), are most feasible, and are within your organization's capabilities to execute.

The participants reviewed the RAIT and saw that seed and seed systems response and crop-related infrastructure response had scores of 3 for the upcoming pre-production and production stages. The organization that led the RAIT (and would implement the response) had significant experience with seed and seed systems projects, but they did not have experience with infrastructure responses. Therefore, the participants agreed to prioritize a seed and seed systems response and highlighted the one priority cell.

Based on the results of the RAIT, the organization would use Chapter 5 to understand the technical options and timing tables, and work through the decision tree to design the response.

The participants recognized the need for an infrastructure response but could not undertake this response. However, they had worked with another organization that focuses on infrastructure, so they would contact that organization to share the results of their RAIT and suggest that an infrastructure response might be appropriate (see SEADS Principle 5).

Appendix 4.3: RAIT template

Figure A4.2: Blank Response-area identification tool (RAIT) template

LIVELIHOOD OBJECTIVES BY RESPONSE AREA	STAGE OF THE CROP PRODUCTION CYCLE DURING WHICH THE RESPONSE WILL OCCUR			
	Pre-production planning (for example, crop or seed selection)	Production (for example, land preparation, crop management)	Post-production (for example, harvesting, storage, processing)	Marketing (for example, market access, transport)
Seed and seed systems (Chapter 5)				
SEADS livelihood objective 1: Provide immediate livelihood benefits				
SEADS livelihood objective 2: Protect essential crop-related livelihoods				
SEADS livelihood objective 3: Rebuild or support crop-related production, infrastructure, and systems to strengthen livelihoods				
Tools, equipment, and other non-seed inputs (Chapter 6)				
SEADS livelihood objective 1: Provide immediate livelihood benefits				
SEADS livelihood objective 2: Protect essential crop-related livelihoods				
SEADS livelihood objective 3: Rebuild or support crop-related production, infrastructure, and systems to strengthen livelihoods				
Crop-related infrastructure (Chapter 7)				
SEADS livelihood objective 1: Provide immediate livelihood benefits				
SEADS livelihood objective 2: Protect essential crop-related livelihoods				
SEADS livelihood objective 3: Rebuild or support crop-related production, infrastructure, and systems to strengthen livelihoods				

Legend for scoring			
3 Significant impact on livelihood objective	**2** Small impact on objective	**1** Very little impact on objective	**n/a** No impact on livelihood objective OR crop production stage is not applicable for your response

Appendix 4.4: The three SEADS response areas can each impact livelihoods

Table A4.1: The three SEADS response areas can each impact livelihoods

Livelihood objectives	Response area and technical options	Minimum project duration
Objective 1: To provide immediate livelihood benefits to crop-producing households affected by crisis	Seed and seed systems • Facilitate access to seed • Provide seed Tools, equipment, and other non-seed inputs • Facilitate access to inputs • Provide inputs Crop-related infrastructure • Facilitate community-led rehabilitation	6 months
Objective 2: To protect crop-related livelihoods of households affected by crisis	Seed and seed systems • Facilitate access to seed • Support seed systems • Provide seed Tools, equipment, and other non-seed inputs • Facilitate access to inputs • Provide inputs • Support formal and informal input systems Crop-related infrastructure • Facilitate community-led rehabilitation • Lead and implement direct infrastructure rehabilitation	6 months

...continued

| Objective 3: To rebuild or support crop-related production, infrastructure, and systems to ensure livelihoods for households affected by crisis | Seed and seed systems
• Facilitate access to seed
• Support seed systems
Tools, equipment, and other non-seed inputs
• Facilitate access to inputs
• Support formal and informal input systems
Crop-related infrastructure
• Facilitate community-led rehabilitation
• Lead and implement direct infrastructure rehabilitation | 9 months |

CHAPTER 5:
SEED AND SEED SYSTEMS

Minimum standards: seed and seed systems

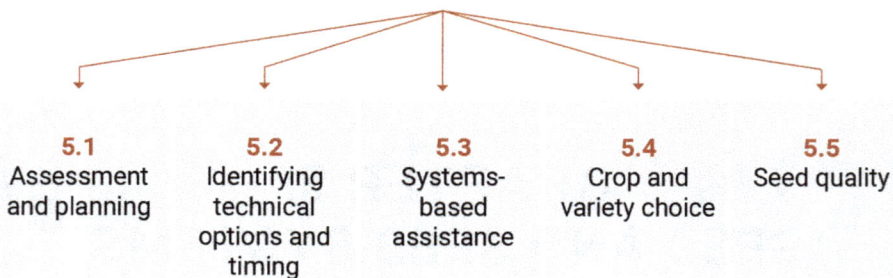

5.1
Assessment and planning

5.2
Identifying technical options and timing

5.3
Systems-based assistance

5.4
Crop and variety choice

5.5
Seed quality

Annex A: Glossary contains definitions of some of the technical terms used in SEADS.

This chapter provides options for assessing, designing, and implementing seed and seed system responses.

Seed includes any plant part, including grains (botanic seeds) and vegetative materials, used to propagate annual, perennial, and horticultural crops. Seed systems are the means through which crop producers access and select the seed or planting material they want and need. These systems include actors that play a role in the research, production, supply, regulation, and certification of seed and planting material. Seed systems can be formal, informal, or integrated.

A crisis affects seed and seed systems in different ways. During a rapid-onset crisis, such as a flood or hurricane, or a complex crisis:

- Availability of, access to, and quality of crop seed and planting material may be affected.
- Stores of saved crop seed may be damaged or lost completely in natural disasters.
- Stores of saved crop seed may be left behind, looted, or destroyed during displacement.
- Private sector activities that supply crop seed to local markets and seed production may be temporarily or permanently abandoned due to insecurity or inaccessibility.

During a slow-onset crisis, such as a drought or pest infestation, existing seed varieties may be found to be unsuitable for the crisis conditions. Access to appropriate varieties becomes a critical part of crop-related crisis response.

Links to the SEADS livelihood objectives

Crisis response that addresses seed and seed systems relates to all three SEADS livelihood objectives:

1. to provide immediate livelihood benefits to crop-producing households affected by crisis.
2. to protect crop-related livelihoods of households affected by crisis.
3. to rebuild or support crop-related production, infrastructure, and systems to ensure livelihoods for households affected by crisis.

If seed is available, accessible, and of suitable quality, crop production can be restored and protected after the crisis and it can continue in early recovery. This provides crop producers and their families with livelihood benefits of food and income (Objectives 1 and 2). Seed and seed system responses can improve preparedness and disaster risk reduction, protecting and strengthening crop production into the future (Objectives 2 and 3).

The importance of seed and seed systems in crisis response

Crops harvested for food and income begin with seed—the most important input for crop producers. For these same crop producers, seed system services can ensure that seed is available, accessible, and of suitable quality. Together, seed and seed systems support seed security, which has an important impact on crop-based livelihoods. Without seed security, crop producers may face reduced or failed harvests and increased hunger and poverty. They may have to sell assets to cope with a lack of food or income. They might be forced to purchase seed for the next season.

The concept of seed security has been used for the last 20 years to assess constraints to and improve crop-related livelihoods (Remington et al. 2002). This concept is adapted in Table 5.1 for use in crisis contexts.

Table 5.1: To assess seed security, assess t hree main constraints

Constraint	Characteristics required for overcoming the constraint	Prevalence in a crisis
Availability	Sufficient quantity of seed of adapted crops is within reasonable proximity (spatial availability) and in time for critical sowing periods (temporal availability)	• Seed is usually available, even after a crisis, though seed availability may be limited in formal channels or in a specific location and time period • In a slow-onset or complex crisis, seed is usually available. Only on rare occasions do these types of crisis prevent markets from providing seed (Rohrbach et al. 2005) • Seed may be unavailable after a rapid-onset crisis, where seed stocks in the region have been destroyed or damaged beyond use and where crop producers procured seed through formal channels • Crop producers often supplement seed received via aid with seed from their stock or own sources (Mollet 2010, FAO 2012a, FAO 2012b)

...continued

		• Crisis-affected households may consume their seed during an acute food security crisis
Access	Producers can acquire the seed that they need and prefer, without: • economic barriers to purchase or barter • physical barriers, including distance to market, security threats, and quarantine • cultural and social barriers, including disabilities, age, gender, ethnicity, and other biases, language gaps, and limited access to information	• In a complex or rapid-onset crisis, crop producers may be unable to afford the seed they need, as they may have lost assets and sources of income • Insecurity can prevent access to markets where seed is purchased • Rapid-onset crises can destroy infrastructure, such as roads, that are needed to get to markets
Seed quality	Seed: • is adapted, productive, and has desired traits (variety quality) • can germinate and develop into a healthy crop (physiological quality) • is free from impurities (physical quality) • is free of diseases or pests (phytosanitary quality) See Minimum Standard 5.5 for more detail	• Seed quality constraints are not often caused by a crisis and are usually chronic (except in pest infestations). SEADS does not cover chronic stress contexts • Seed available in a crisis is often not from formal channels and its quality may not be ideal. However, it may still be selected and used by producers (Sperling et al. 2020)

Seed and seed system responses are most likely to impact livelihoods when constraints are correctly identified and addressed. The *Minimum Technical Standards for Seed System Assessment in Emergencies* (FAO et al. 2020) and the *Seed Emergency Response Tool* (Sperling et al. 2022) can help identify constraints by crop that exist for households affected by crisis. Where assessment determines that seed security is not a problem, a seed response may not be necessary, and development and resilience programming may be more appropriate (Bramel et al. 2004).

Other essential inputs and infrastructure assets are often needed to ensure that planted seeds result in food, income, and other livelihood impacts. An approach that combines seed and non-seed responses may be necessary to achieve livelihood objectives. For example, the SEADS (2021) evidence review found some evidence that direct seed distribution combined with the provision of fertilizer, irrigation equipment, tools, and/or training resulted in either higher levels of food security, reduction in food expenditures, or additional income (FAO 2012a, FAO 2012b, World Bank 2012, Pretari & Anguko 2019, Cullis 2020).

Technical options for supporting seed and seed systems

Seed and seed system responses are common in every type of crisis, and across all agro-ecological zones and farming systems. This chapter presents three technical options and several sub-options for ensuring seed security in a crisis:

- facilitate access to seed
- support seed systems
- provide seed.

The technical options assume that if crop producers lack suitable seed to plant, providing them with seed will enable them to produce food or income. This assumes that crop producers have access to other production inputs, that agro-climatic conditions and the security context are favorable to crop production, and that the food produced can be stored until it is consumed or sold.

Case Study 5.1 (see SEADS website) provides an example of seed and tool provision resulting in extra months of food self-sufficiency.

These three technical options were selected based on available evidence of impact from agriculture responses in humanitarian crisis (SEADS 2021) and on expert opinion. However, evidence did not disaggregate what caused the impact on livelihoods when a combination of seed and non-seed response areas and technical options was used to address all identified constraints.

Evidence indicates that combinations of technical options can improve livelihood outcomes, either through increased food security, reduced food expenditures, or increased income. See for example Mollet 2010, FAO 2012a, FAO 2012b, World Bank 2012, Pretari & Anguko 2019, and Cullis 2020 in the *SEADS Evidence Database*.

Case Study 5.2 (see SEADS website) focuses on seed systems issues in crisis and provides example of linking the type of seed security constraint with the response area selected.

Technical options related to tools, equipment, and other non-seed inputs are discussed in Chapter 6: Tools, Equipment, and Other Non-seed Inputs. Crop-related infrastructure responses are discussed in Chapter 7: Crop-related Infrastructure. Common responses that may be appropriate to combine with a seed response are listed in Table 6.3 and Table 7.1.

Technical Option 1: Facilitate access to seed

This refers to any market-aware action that helps crop producers get seeds in time for planting. It excludes direct distribution of seed, which is covered under Technical Option 3: Provide seed. Before, during, or after a crisis, access to seed can be rapidly facilitated in many ways depending on the context.

Access to seed can motivate crisis-affected households to restart crop production. If the minimum standards in this chapter are achieved, it can also allow them to increase their crop production. Several examples of market-aware (or market-based) sub-options that address the three barriers to access (see Table 5.1) are listed in Table 5.2.

Case Study 5.3 (see SEADS website) shows how voucher assistance has been used alongside food assistance and the impact the combination had on livelihoods.

Table 5.2: Several technical sub-options are available to address seed access constraints

Technical sub-options	Access constraints		
	Economic	Physical	Sociocultural
1.1. Provide cash to targeted participants so they can buy suitable seed that is available in local markets	x		
1.2. Provide cash to targeted participants so they can use safe transportation to markets to buy seed	x		
1.3. Provide cash to seed sellers or physically transport them closer to targeted participants (for example, seed fairs)		x	x
1.4. Provide cash grants or credit to seed sellers to move supplies to remote areas		x	x

Technical Option 2: Support for the seed system

Seed system activities are those that support the actors in the seed supply chain. In normal times, where crop production plays a primary role in livelihoods, state and non-state systems and services ensure that crop producers have the seed they need to produce, harvest, and market crops. These systems include both government and private actors that have a role in the research, production, supply, sale, regulation, and certification of seed and planting material.

Crises can often disrupt those systems or weaken already weak systems further without destroying them completely. Support to the seed system can be rapid and address availability and quality constraints. Support to seed systems can improve them by strengthening formal and informal sellers' and state actors' ability to cover the required seed demand before, during, and after a crisis. This support can encourage early recovery and economic growth and ensure future production, thus decreasing dependence on repeated cycles of aid. Several examples of sub-options that address the availability and quality constraints described in Table 5.1 are listed in Table 5.3.

Table 5.3: Several sub-options are available to support the seed system

Technical sub-options	Availability constraints		Seed quality constraints
	Physical	Temporal	
2.1. Raise crop producers' and seed sellers' awareness of seed quality			x
2.2. Provide cash support to formal and informal seed multipliers to produce seed for future seasons. Often used for tubers (for example, sweet potatoes)	x		x
2.3. Provide credit or loan guarantees to local seed sellers to buy seed for humanitarian tenders		x	x
2.4. Provide technical assistance to seed multipliers or sellers to improve quantity and quality of their planting material	x		x
2.5. Provide technical assistance and funding to establish community seed banks	x	x	

Case Study 5.4 (see SEADS website) provides practical examples of supply-side, market-led support in the formal seed sector, with the goal of ensuring availability of improved seed varieties.

Technical Option 3: Provide seed

Direct seed distribution (DSD) provides seed directly to crop producers in time for them to plant for the targeted cropping seasons. DSD may also introduce improved varieties or certified seed that beneficiaries are familiar with, but which are not available locally. It can also renew lost or damaged seed stocks from the same improved seed variety.

DSD is only suitable when seed is unavailable and markets are not functioning, a rare context even in a crisis. In this rare context, without DSD, no seed of any quality would be available to plant.

DSD often reflects food distribution models in that seed is procured and brought to the crisis-affected area. Targeted participants gather in central locations to receive their allotted seed for free.

Advantages and disadvantages of each technical option

The advantages and disadvantages of each technical option for supporting seed and seed systems are summarized in Table 5.4.

Table 5.4: Each technical option has advantages and disadvantages

Option	Advantages	Disadvantages
1. Facilitate access to seed	• Rapid, except seed fairs • Supports crop producer-determined priorities and choice of crops and varieties • Cash injected into local formal and informal economies • Can be done face to face (direct cash) or using digital transfers	• Cash provided may not be used for seed as crop producers have many competing priorities • Seed quality control may be weak depending on sellers participating, requiring sufficient market and agronomic competencies (see Annex B) to monitor

...continued

	• Bolsters all seed systems crop producers use, formal and informal, and has greater long-term impact (Rohrbach et al. 2005, Sperling et al. 2008, McGuire & Sperling 2013) • Can be designed to support women's role in seed sale and marketing system • Seed choice can be tracked to inform future responses (Henderson & Herby 2019)	that sufficient good-quality seed of the right variety is consistently available • Seed fairs can be labor intensive to organize and implement, may only reach a relatively small number of crop producers, and cannot be done if people cannot congregate • When using vouchers, benefits to informal seed systems may be limited if informal sellers are excluded in favor of sellers who are registered or carry only certified seed
2. Support seed systems	• Naturally aligns with SEADS Principle 2 • Offers an exit strategy for organizations trying to break repeated cycles of aid • Creates inclusive business relationships between value-chain actors • Builds on existing community strengths • Favors coordination and links to development efforts (SEADS Principle 5)	• Requires sufficient market and supply chain knowledge to avoid creating artificial markets, as with sweet potato vine multiplication, for instance, that has no real market beyond relief (see Annex B) • If program requirements allow only formal sellers and state actors, informal sellers and systems may be undermined

	• Links research results with extension and communities • Strengthens local seed certification and regulation processes • Strengthens availability of improved varieties	• May require more time for initial assessment if target systems are not already known and understood
3. Provide seed	• Familiar to donors, affected people, and implementers • Logistically relatively easy for implementer • Can reach large populations • Can control initial seed quality (if certification regimes, or rigorous controls by implementers, are in place) • Easily quantifiable in terms of amount of seed distributed and number of clients served • In some settings may be cost-effective if routine sellers are spread out and remote from crop producer aid recipients • Easier to monitor as standard output indicators are used as well as baselines and targets	• Range of crops and varieties on offer and choice among them are limited. Range may not be those most suitable to address stress • Quantities of seeds given may be fixed or not tailored to the specific preferences and needs of each crop producer • Unregistered crop varieties may not be allowed • May undermine markets, both formal and informal • After controlling for quality, seed often arrives to crop producers late • May have challenging transport logistics, including the need for additional trucking and warehouse capacity associated with centralized procurement

...continued

- May support a competitive nascent seed sector and even informal markets and sellers when combined with small lot tenders (for example, a 2-ton limit per tender per crop and variety profile) and preference for local sellers

- Done repeatedly, it can alter local crop and diversity profiles
- Often done repeatedly, it creates crop producer dependency
- Contract delays are common

Timing of seed and seed systems technical options

Timing of seed and seed system technical options should be influenced predominantly by the agriculture calendar and the selected option, as shown in Table 5.5.

Table 5.5: Different seed and seed system technical options are relevant at different stages of the agriculture calendar

TECHNICAL OPTIONS	STAGE OF THE CROP PRODUCTION CYCLE DURING WHICH THE RESPONSE WILL OCCUR			
	Pre-production planning (for example, crop or seed selection)	**Production** (for example, land preparation, crop management)	**Post-production** (for example, harvesting, storage, processing)	**Marketing** (for example, market access, transport)
Facilitate access to seed	⟶			⟶
Support seed systems		⟶		
Provide seed	⟶			

A seed or seed system response must be completed in time for crop producers to have seed in hand before the accepted sowing season for that crop in that location. Any delay beyond the optimal sowing date means less production for crop producers. For example, each week of delay reduced wheat yields by 4.2% in

Syria (van Duivenbooden et al. 2000). With climate change, crop producers' optimal sowing date may be different (and earlier) than in the past (Waha et al. 2013). When facilitating access to seed includes support to seed sellers or other value-chain actors, this support is most relevant when it begins well in advance of the sowing season, and as early as harvest, storage, and handling of the previous season. It is not suitable to facilitate access to seed or provide seed during production or post-production, as they are not needed at this time and may be consumed or sold. Technical options that support the seed system are more flexible and can be considered during any point in the agriculture calendar.

Depending on the location and cultural traditions of crop producers, the cycle of planning, production, post-production, and marketing may repeat as many as three times in one calendar year. Different crops may be sown during different cycles. Often there is a main season when staple crops with longer growth cycles—such as corn, beans, or wheat—are planted and a shorter secondary season when short-cycle crops—such as vegetables—are cultivated.

The crop production stage is generally more relevant to a seed or seed system response than the type of crisis, due to the time-bound nature of crop production. However, the type and phase of the crisis influence the timing of different technical options, as shown in Table 5.6.

Table 5.6: Different seed and seed system technical options are relevant at different phases of a crisis response

TECHNICAL OPTIONS	Rapid-onset crisis				Slow-onset crisis			
	Preparedness	Immediate aftermath	Early recovery	Recovery	Alert	Alarm	Emergency	Recovery
Facilitate access to seed	→→→		→→→		→→→			→→→
Support seed systems	→→→→→→→→→→→→→→→→→→→→→→→				→→→→→→→→→→→→→→→→→→→→→→→			
Provide seed	→→→		→→→					

In a rapid-onset crisis, all three technical options can be done during preparedness if access to program participants may be cut off or income shocks are likely. They can also all be done during early recovery if there is alignment with the agriculture calendar. Technical options that facilitate access to or provide seed should not be done in the immediate aftermath of a rapid-onset crisis, unless the optimal sowing date of a crop critical to food security and livelihoods will occur before early recovery.

In a slow-onset crisis, it is highly unlikely that seed availability constraints require seed to be provided. However, constraints related to seed quality, or other weaknesses in the prevailing seed system, may trigger the need to facilitate access or support and strengthen the seed system.

The recovery phase of either a rapid- or slow-onset crisis is not a suitable time to consider providing seed. During recovery, the seed system will be capable of resolving any seed availability constraints.

Decision tree to select technical options

A decision tree can guide your choice of technical options. It prompts you to consider the variables in a systematic way. Decision tree questions are ordered in terms of priority to program quality.

Answer Question 1 first (either "yes" or "no"). The decision tree directs you to a new question based on your answer. "No" responses indicate that other suitable responses identified in the RAIT should be considered or that further training or capacity building may be required to answer "yes" to the questions. As multiple technical options may be appropriate, when one technical option has been selected, the decision tree will lead you to consideration of others.

Answers should be based on all data at your disposal, but in particular:

- the results of the initial assessment (see Chapter 4: Initial Assessment for Crop-related Crisis Response)
- a theory of change (see Minimum Standard 8.2: Project objectives)
- your organization's capacity to achieve relevant minimum standards in this chapter (see Annex B).

SEADS recommends that you complete a RAIT (see Minimum Standard 4.4: Selecting response areas) before completing a decision tree. The RAIT will indicate whether seed and seed system responses are necessary, appropriate, and feasible, and which livelihood objective they may have the greatest impact on.

Use Figure 5.1 to test whether seed and seed systems should be part of a crop-related response and, if so, which technical options will be most appropriate.

Figure 5.1: Decision tree for seed and seed systems

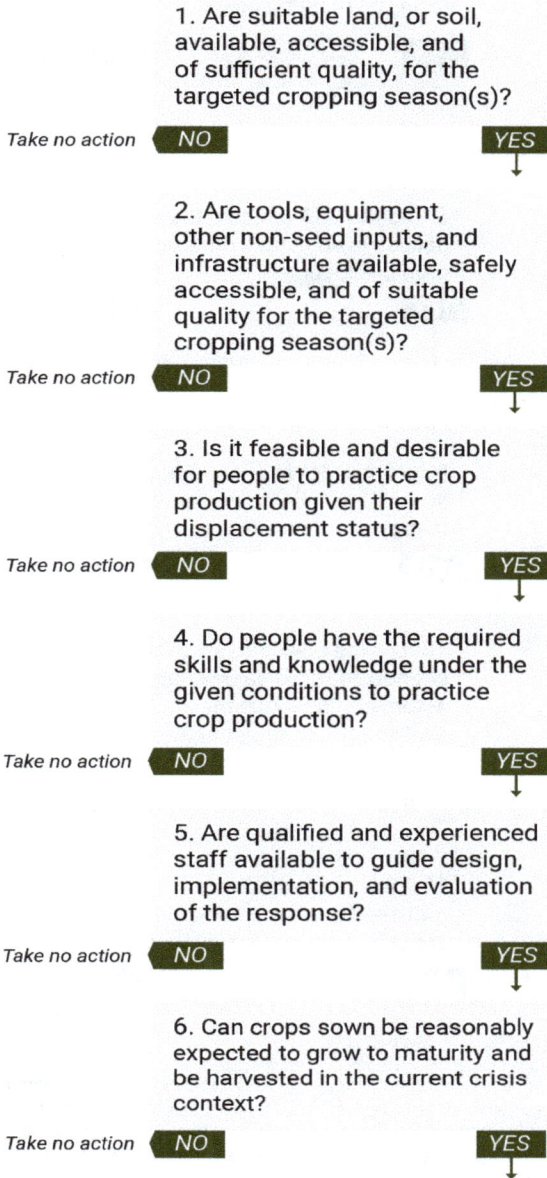

1. Are suitable land, or soil, available, accessible, and of sufficient quality, for the targeted cropping season(s)?

Take no action **NO** **YES**

2. Are tools, equipment, other non-seed inputs, and infrastructure available, safely accessible, and of suitable quality for the targeted cropping season(s)?

Take no action **NO** **YES**

3. Is it feasible and desirable for people to practice crop production given their displacement status?

Take no action **NO** **YES**

4. Do people have the required skills and knowledge under the given conditions to practice crop production?

Take no action **NO** **YES**

5. Are qualified and experienced staff available to guide design, implementation, and evaluation of the response?

Take no action **NO** **YES**

6. Can crops sown be reasonably expected to grow to maturity and be harvested in the current crisis context?

Take no action **NO** **YES**

(Continued on next page)

7. Has seed system assessment (SSA) been completed?

NO

Use Minimum Technical Standards for Seed System Assessments in Emergencies to complete an SSA and then continue to #8

YES

8. Did the SSA indicate that seed access is an acute constraint to crop production?

NO

YES

Faciliate access to seed and continue to #9 as multiple technical options may be appropriate

9. Did the SSA indicate that seed availability is an acute constraint to crop production?

Go to question #11 NO

YES

10. Did the SSA indicate that support for seed value-chain actors could reduce the acute availability constraint in the targeted season(s)?

Provide seed NO

YES *Support seed systems*

11. Did the SSA indicate that seed quality is an acute constraint to crop production?

Take no action NO

YES *Support seed systems*

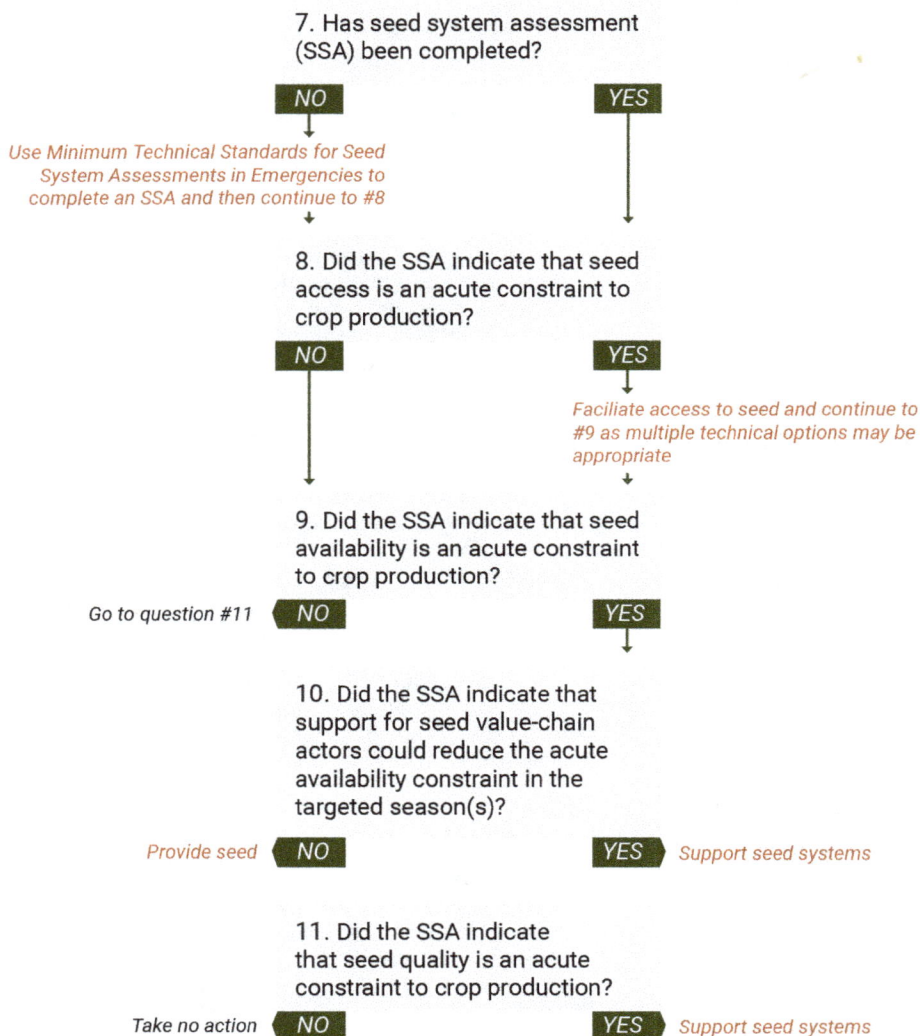

Note: The result *Take no action* does not necessarily mean that no response should take place, but rather that other suitable responses identified in the RAIT should be considered or further training or capacity building may be required to answer "yes" to the questions. Where no other suitable options exist and training and capacity building is not possible, support to alternative livelihoods can be considered.

Seed and seed system minimum standards

Minimum Standard 5.1: Assessment and planning

Assessment determines the seed security constraint(s), market functionality, and needs.

Key actions

- Use the *Minimum Technical Standards for Seed System Assessment in Emergencies* (FAO et al. 2020) to identify seed security constraints (see Guidance notes 1 and 2).

- Ensure seed security assessment (SSA) is participatory and meets SEADS Principle 2: Use a participatory approach in all aspects of crisis response (see Guidance note 3).

- Use Appendix 4.1 and Appendix 5.1 to select assessment questions.

- Identify acute and chronic seed security constraints and link with development programs to address chronic constraints (see Guidance note 4).

- Ensure staff have relevant technical competencies and provide training to fill gaps (see Annex B).

Case Study 5.5 (see SEADS website) demonstrates how assessment and planning are critical to achieving livelihood impacts in vegetable seed responses.

Guidance notes

1. **Food security versus seed security**. It is common in crisis response to use food security assessment as a proxy for seed security, but the two are quite different. A household may be food insecure, but still retain seed for future planting. A SSA considers seed security specifically, by considering the main channels crop producers use to obtain seed for key crops and how well these channels are functioning in a crisis setting. SSAs consider four seed security constraints: seed availability, accessibility, health, and varietal suitability. The *Minimum Technical Standards for Seed System Assessment in Emergencies*

suggest elements to include in your assessment, as well as suggested methods and processes (FAO et al. 2020). An SSA is the first step in the design and planning of your seed and seed system support response (FAO 2016).

2.   **Formal and informal seed channels**. Crop producers rely on both formal and informal systems to achieve seed security. The formal system operates through government, commercial companies, or humanitarian channels, and offers improved varieties of a few key crops. Seed offered through the formal system is typically certified and of reliable quality. However, the formal system is often challenging for smallholders to access due to distance and minimum purchase requirements. The informal system provides seed from producers' own harvest (called *farmers' varieties* or *landraces*), social networks, and local markets. It offers different seed quality and price points, although quality claims tend to be less reliable than in the formal system.

Crop producers may use multiple channels for procuring their seed out of necessity, benefit-cost concerns, and preference. These channels may differ by crop. For instance, some crop producers may access hybrid maize seed from agro-dealers, but common bean from own stocks or local markets. Others may source vegetable seed from an agro-dealer and sorghum from own stocks or neighbors. Multiple channels may be used for a single crop. For example, producers may source some bean seed from own stocks and some from local markets, supplemented by new improved varieties from research. A breakdown in formal channels during a crisis may therefore affect some crops, but those sourced through informal channels may be unaffected. Note also that crop producers use different channels in a crisis. For instance, when they lose their own seed stocks, crop producers may use local markets to supplement their seed supply. It is important to assess how all these channels function together. A common mistake is to assess supply only from the formal sector channels, ignoring the contributions of informal seed channels that may be especially important during a crisis. An SSA differentiates between different channels and considers crop producers' needs and preferences. An SSA should give you an understanding of the characteristics of acute and chronic seed security constraints and allow you to identify a response strategy and programming plan (see Minimum Standard 5.2).

Case Study 5.6 (see SEADS website) draws evidence from SSAs done in different contexts. It shows that while formal seed systems help producers withstand and recover from future shocks, informal systems are often more important, particularly for local markets and sellers.

3.   **Participation**. Each crop, crop producer, and crop-producing region differs both agro-ecologically and anthropologically. Understanding these differences can significantly improve program quality and impact. A participatory approach that

engages both those that demand (i.e., are in need of) seed and those that supply seed can identify these nuances. For example, participants can share the coping mechanisms they use regarding where and how they obtain seed in a crisis, or why they plant in a particular pattern, or why they prefer a particular crop when they are faced with insecurity. Active engagement from project participants in the SSA can identify preferred markets and why, and which ones are functioning better than others. See SEADS Principle 2 for guidance on ensuring effective participation in your assessments and Chapter 4 for methods and tools to support participation.

4. **Acute versus chronic constraints.** Assessment can reveal both acute and chronic seed insecurity, as they often exist together where crises are common. Acute seed insecurity is brought on by distinct, short-term events that can affect a broad range of the population. It can be spurred by failure to plant, loss of a harvest, or high pest infestation in storage. Chronic seed insecurity is independent of a specific crisis, although it may be exacerbated by it. Chronic seed insecurity may occur in populations who have been marginalized economically, ecologically, or politically. Crisis response is not well suited to address these chronic problems directly. Nevertheless, humanitarian organizations have a responsibility to understand these chronic problems so as not to exacerbate them. When chronic constraints are identified in the decision tree in Figure 5.1, this can be a signal to share information and collaborate on program design with early recovery and development programs and host governments. This collaboration can provide a forum in which to share knowledge of chronic seed security constraints identified through SSAs, and to raise awareness of how crop-related crisis response may exacerbate chronic constraints.

Minimum Standard 5.2: Identifying technical options and timing

Selected technical option(s) alleviate the seed security constraints identified by the SSA, consider market-aware responses, and are completed in time for crisis-affected households to have seed in hand for the sowing season.

Key actions

- Use the decision tree in Figure 5.1 to select appropriate technical options given the identified constraints; where possible, favor market-based response options (see Guidance note 1).

- Use participatory approaches to confirm that the technical options are acceptable to crop producers (see SEADS Principle 2, Chapter 4, and Appendix 5.1).
- Base the scale of assistance on appropriate targeting, real-time costs, sowing rates, and access to assets (see Guidance notes 2 and 3).
- For the technical options chosen, devise a timeline from delivery date backward and assess bottlenecks for the potential to delay delivery beyond a useful date (see Guidance note 4).

Guidance notes

1.   Constraints and security context alignment. If seed and seed system responses do not explicitly mitigate identified seed security constraints, crop-related crisis responses can jeopardize households' ability to produce food or earn income. For example, if in a specific zone seeds are provided or access is facilitated year after year, crop producers and markets become dependent on humanitarian funding to function. In these circumstances, rather than repeated emergency seed distributions, linking with development programs to help crop producers generate income or find alternative livelihoods can be useful.

People affected by crisis have to feel confident that the situation is stable and secure enough for them to cultivate, harvest, fully process, and market their crops. If seed is provided in an unstable or insecure situation, it may encourage displaced populations to return to farming before the risk is removed or before they are fully comfortable doing so. This would be undesirable in many situations, such as in areas affected by conflict or with active landmines.

The decision tree (see Figure 5.1) and Minimum Standard 5.1 provide guidance on how to ensure that your selected technical response has the potential to alleviate identified seed security constraints. SEADS Principle 1 provides information on market-based responses.

2.   Targeting. A participant selection process (Weatherall 2019), using simple selection criteria, and information sharing between humanitarian actors are crucial to target the most vulnerable crop-producing households (Rohrbach et al. 2005). See Minimum Standard 4.4 for more detail on targeting.

3.   Scale of assistance. Once a technical option is selected, determine the scale of assistance required. For example, estimate factors such as the cash needed to facilitate access to seed and the amount of seed needed to address availability constraints. Align the scale of assistance with livelihood targets, such as specific levels of income from crop sales or specific levels of food consumption. Consider the cost of services, such as transportation, that are needed to access seed, and the cost of seed itself. Use that information either to budget for procurement or to convert into a cash value for a market-based response (see SEADS Principle 1). Knowledge of historical prices can help with these calculations, but in a crisis costs can fluctuate dramatically and rapidly. *MERS Asset Distribution Standard 1* provides useful guidance and tools. *MISMA Key Action 5: Market Monitoring* provides guidance on monitoring costs and adapting programs when needed.

Calculations of how much seed to provide also rely on an understanding of realistic sowing rates and average surface area cultivated in each community. Participatory assessment and design activities can help corroborate suitable sowing rates and surface areas. Indeed, crop producers are not only seed consumers and users, but also seed producers and seed managers. Even when free seed is provided, in most cases crop producers also plant seed from their stock or own sources (Mollet 2010, FAO 2012a, FAO 2012b). Direct observation of a representative sample of active (not fallow) fields can provide a realistic gauge of how much land households are capable of seeding, maintaining, and harvesting. Where direct observation is not possible, interviews with knowledgeable crop producers and field-based value-chain actors can serve as a proxy. For example, seed sellers might know how much seed households buy on average each year by crop.

It is rare that 100% of seed or transportation costs is needed. Knowledge of target participants' coping strategies can determine whether households may still have some assets with which to meet their needs. For example, in temporary, short-term displacements, people may be able to take their seed stores or savings with them. In all of these calculations, vulnerability dynamics will influence calculations of need, and an understanding of these dynamics is essential to a rights-based approach. Appendix 5.1 provides guiding questions to ensure calculations of assistance are equitable and realistic.

4.   Oft-repeated bottlenecks. Seed and seed system responses often face with common bottlenecks that can jeopardize their livelihood impacts. In a complex crisis, where security is uncertain, crop producers may delay land preparation until they have seed in hand. In this case, timelines for delivery dates of cash or seed need to be calculated to include time for land preparation, not just to the latest planting date. For DSD, there are often problems with contract delays, seed quality checks, and import permits. For voucher programs, frequent bottlenecks arise with printing processes and screening sellers. For seed fairs, there are often delays in fair planning and logistics and e-voucher set-up. Previous project reports, participation from crisis-affected crop producers, and coordination with other organizations can help illuminate the most common bottlenecks for the target area and type of response.

Minimum Standard 5.3: Systems-based assistance

Market-based seed and seed system support is aligned with a livelihoods-based approach and supports systems, services, and markets that support crop-based livelihoods.

Key actions

- Use a livelihoods-based approach to guide market-based seed and seed system responses (see Guidance note 1).
- Ensure seed responses encourage producer choice of seed (see Guidance note 2).
- Ensure seed responses leverage local and existing seed sources (see Guidance note 3).
- Ensure seed responses create healthy competition among sellers or sources of seed (see Guidance note 4).
- Ensure seed responses support systems that are accountable to crop producers (see Guidance note 5).

Guidance notes

1. **Livelihoods approach.** Under a livelihoods approach to seed and seed system responses, assistance programs consider all components that link seed to livelihoods (see SEADS Principle 1). For example, suitable land access is necessary to realize any benefits from seed responses. Can the available seed thrive in the type of land accessible to crop producers? Can that access be safely assured from the time of land preparation until harvest? Another critical link between seed and livelihoods is through pre-existing systems, services, and markets such as seed multipliers and sellers. For example, prior to the crisis, which sellers did crop producers use for seed? Have these sellers been affected by the crisis, and can they still provide seed? How well are the markets functioning? Assessment tools,

such as the *Emergency Market Mapping and Analysis Toolkit* (Albu 2010), when focused on the seed value-chain can highlight the strengths and weaknesses of seed-related systems, services, and markets.

2.   **Producer choice of seed.** Producers prioritize crop and source by considering factors such as end use of the crop, distance to sellers, risk, labor availability, and cash or credit availability. Market-based programs with the greatest level of choice are most likely to effectively meet crop producers' needs and have an impact on livelihoods. However, the greater the choice, the more complicated the logistics of screening and integrating seed sellers. When given complete free choice, through unconditional cash, experience has shown that even when SSAs show that there is an economic access constraint to seed, participants will spend a portion of their assistance on non-seed items. A good cash-for-seed response considers that people have other needs, focuses on useful seed choices, and may provide a larger transfer value to make sure people are meeting basic needs, or it may provide cash for seed in conjunction with lifesaving responses. Case Study 5.3 (see SEADS website) provides an example of producers making the best-use choice in a voucher and seed fair approach.

3.   **Local and existing seed sources.** Seed can be procured from outside the agro-ecological region in which a crisis occurs, or it can be procured from the affected region itself. Procuring local seed within the affected region may support the local economy. However, market-based purchases may overlook functioning informal seed systems. For example, crop producers often store and manage their own seed. They typically share and access seed based on kinship and social relations. Informal systems supply the bulk of off-farm seed and are an important seed source for poorer crop producers. They offer a diversity of seed for varied crops and varieties, including open-pollinated varieties (particularly common bean and groundnut). Cash and voucher-based assistance can often overlook, downplay, or directly work against functioning informal systems. Some local seed markets use bartering, not cash, so participants in those markets will not benefit from cash transfers. Where informal local sellers are weaker than formal sellers, it may be possible to improve the functionality of the seed system by supporting seed sellers in conjunction with explicit market-based approaches; for example, by providing training on safe storage of seed or seed quality.

4.   **Competition.** Competition between sellers or sources of seed can keep prices from inflating when demand increases. While local market seed prices normally increase at the start of the sowing period, competition can moderate such price changes. At the same time, competition also incentivizes sellers to offer better quality in order to attract new customers. In addition, having multiple providers can

increase the range of crops and varieties offered, with a higher likelihood that these will meet crop producers' preferences and be well adapted to their growing conditions. Effective competition for price, quality, and selection within market systems allows crop producers to make better choices.

5. **Accountability.** Value-chain actors who operate throughout the year in the targeted areas have strong incentives to be accountable, as they may offer other goods and services to crop producers and have reputations to maintain. Participatory planning and implementation of system-based assistance allows stakeholders to agree on processes for handling complaints about seed quality, and for publicizing these procedures. If a seed seller benefits from system support, their goal is to get a share of the market or be established as a trusted source of suitable seed at a specific location. Consequently, they must be accountable for the products they sell to crop producers in order to ensure a sustainable market position and customer base. If seed sellers are contracted (often through DSD, fairs, or vouchers), measures should be in place to ensure seed quality and to penalize any seller of poor-quality seed.

Minimum Standard 5.4: Crop and variety choice

The crops and varieties involved in the response are suitable for the context: adapted, usable under crop producers' management, and deemed acceptable by producers.

Key actions

- Confirm producer and gender preferences, donor and host government acceptability, and ecological suitability of selected crops for the targeted season (see Guidance notes 1, 2, and 3).

- Document your process for confirming that varieties are acceptable to targeted growers and can be productive under their management conditions. Consider open-pollinated varieties (see Guidance note 4).

- Ensure that an array of crops and varieties are included in the options on offer (see Guidance note 5).

Guidance notes

1. **Livelihood objectives.** If the targeted livelihood goal of the response is to provide immediate benefits to producers, long-cycle crops, such as cassava or fruit trees, may not be appropriate.

2. **Household preferences.** Crop producers sow different crops and varieties. Especially when facing high stress, households may intensify certain strategies and dramatically alter others. Producers benefit from flexible crop and variety choice so they can tailor sowing needs to their own household needs (incorporating men's and women's preferences). In confirming crop producers' preferences, focus on both consumption traits (like taste and cooking time) and sale traits. Women and men may assess traits differently, with women emphasizing household needs and men focusing on traits needed for marketing.

3. **Choice and suitability.** In direct seed responses, the distributed varieties (open-pollinated varieties versus hybrid or local versus globally purchased seeds) must be appropriate for the agro-ecological conditions and local crop production practices (Buruchura et al. 2002, Haugen & Fowler 2003, Pincus et al. 2017, McGuire & Sperling 2013). A crisis can provide an opportunity to introduce crop types or varieties that may be more suitable for the changing climate. In many countries, use of genetically modified organisms may be restricted by the government or avoided by crop producers. Understanding the legality of genetically modified organisms in the program area can avoid undesired delays in implementation and ensure acceptability of crop choice and variety.

Case Study 5.7 (see SEADS website) shows how a suitable crop choice has helped crop producers to maintain production in the remaining period of the rainy season.

4. **Local (farmers' varieties or landraces) or modern (improved) varieties.** Varieties offered may be local or modern, depending on crop producers' needs, wants, and prior experience. In a crisis response, do not introduce varieties that have not been previously tested in the area with crop producers' involvement. Support for improved varieties that have been tested locally can encourage local seed production and knowledge transfer. When combined with support to local sellers and seed producers, this support can raise the profile of landraces and crop producers' preferred varieties. Seed in small packets allows crop producers to test unfamiliar seed varieties with minimal risk to overall production.

5. **Realistic management conditions.** Crops and varieties should be shown to perform well under routine and realistic producer management conditions, not only

under ideal growing conditions with purchased inputs. Formal seed-sector regulations tend to encourage varietal purity. However, crop producers often consume their own harvest, sell it locally, or sow in a risk-prone and variable environment. For these uses, purity might be less important. Self- and open-pollinated varieties are often preferred for crisis responses because crop producers can save the seed from the harvest to plant in the following season. Hybrid varieties of field crops are generally not recommended for crisis responses as crop producers have to repurchase seed if they continue sowing that variety. Hybrids should be considered only where people affected by crisis have prior experience with hybrids, such as in horticulture, can independently source them, and explicitly want them.

Minimum Standard 5.5: Seed quality

The quality of the seed in the response meets the needs and requirements of crop-producing communities, practitioners, and donor organizations.

Key actions

- Decide on seed quality criteria to be met and justify why these criteria have been chosen (see Guidance notes 1 and 2).

- Confirm that the quality is at least as good as what crop producers routinely use, and that it is acceptable to farming communities, donors, authorities, and practitioners (see Guidance notes 1 and 2).

- Allow sufficient time to check seed quality against requirements prior to procurement. Be prepared to reject bad-quality seed (see Guidance note 3).

- Decide if seed should be treated with pesticides or fungicides (and why). If there is packaging, ensure that labels and instructions are intelligible locally (see Guidance note 4).

Guidance notes

1. **Aspects of seed quality.** Seed quality is important for all crop types. It is particularly important for vegetatively propagated crops, in which the planting material is not a grain but a vegetative part of the plant (stem, root, vine, sucker) (FAO 2010a). It is also important for saplings in tree-based responses. A primary

concern about using these materials in crisis responses is that pests and diseases might be present on or in the living tissue of vegetative planting materials. These can be transmitted when transported to other areas, where they can potentially infect not only the crop but other species as well. Participation of project participants in the assessment of seed quality can ensure that seed that is provided or available in the market is of acceptable quality because they know the source and the practices used for plant multiplication and selection of planting material. This type of participation has led to the understanding that groundnuts retain the best quality if they are provided in their shells, despite the added labor for project participants. It is important to note, however, that seed quality alone does not mean that seed will grow in an area and that crop producers will want it. The genetic quality desired by crop producers also has to be met. The *Voluntary Guide for National Seed Policy Formulation* (FAO 2015) details different types of quality indicators, such as truth in labeling, certification, quality-declared seed, and non-certified seed.

2.   **Avoiding stereotypes.** Many practitioners and donors define quality according to the formal sector definition and equate quality with certified seed. However, certified improved seed is not always good quality, especially once it reaches the crop producer. Conversely, some producer-saved seed (farmers' varieties/landraces) may be of fine quality. In addition, poor storage or transport conditions can affect seed quality. Other seed quality assurance can expand seed offerings beyond certified seed (see Guidance notes 3 and 4).

3.   **Meeting quality criteria.** Seed quality must be sufficient to result in strong, reliable production. It must also be free of seed-borne pathogens that could spread and infect non-aid seed stocks and neighboring fields. Appendix 5.2 suggests indicators and typical targets for meeting seed quality criteria. See FAO (2010b) for detailed information on evaluating seed quality. The International Seed Testing Association sets out internationally recognized seed quality testing rules (ISTA 2022). Where seed testing may not be feasible, a visual inspection (adapted from indicators in Appendix 5.2) may be sufficient.

4.   **Treatment and labeling.** Seed treatment against pests, such as fungi, may be necessary to ensure procured stocks of seed maintain their quality until they are distributed. Warn recipients of such seed that it is toxic and therefore inedible. There can be a disconnect between the label and the quality of seed delivered to crop producers if the quality deteriorates in storage or during transport. Germination rates at the sites of distribution can provide a minimum of assurance that quality has survived transport.

Recommended reading

Details of references cited in this chapter are in Annex C. Further recommended reading includes:

Berti, P.R., Krasevec, J. & FitzGerald, S. (2004). A review of the effectiveness of agriculture interventions in improving nutrition outcomes. *Public Health Nutrition 7*, 599–609. https://doi.org/10.1079/PHN2003595

Buruchara, R., Sperling, L., Ewell, P. & Kirkby, R. (2002). The role of research institutions in seed-related disaster relief: Seeds of Hope experiences in Rwanda. *Disasters 26*, 288–301. https://doi.org/10.1111/1467-7717.00207

Byrne, K. (2022). *Resources to strengthen adaptive management for livelihoods programming in emergency settings.* Mercy Corps (as part of the Strengthening Capacity in Agriculture, Livelihoods, and Environment (SCALE) Associate Award). https://www.fsnnetwork.org/resource/resources-strengthen-adaptive-management-livelihoods-programming-emergency-settings

Food and Agriculture Organization (FAO) (2006). *Quality-declared seed system.* FAO Plant Production and Protection Paper 185. http://www.fao.org/3/a0503e/a0503e00.htm

FAO (1999). *Restoring farmers' seed systems in disaster situations.* Plant Production and Protection Paper #150. FAO.

Iannotti, L., Cunningham, K. & Ruel, M. (2009). *Improving diet quality and micronutrient nutrition: Homestead food production in Bangladesh.* International Food Policy Research Institute.

Keane, J., Brick, G. & Sperling, L. (2019). *Study on cash transfers for seed security in humanitarian settings.* A Feed the Future Global Supporting Seed Systems for Development activity (S34D) report. https://hdl.handle.net/10568/107948

Mollet, M. (2009). *Emergency support for the restoration of food security in the areas of southern Myanmar affected by Cyclone Nargis: Beneficiaries results assessment (BRA) survey.* Unpublished. FAO.

Olney, D.K., Pedehombga, A., Ruel, M.T. & Dillon, A. (2015). A 2-year integrated agriculture and nutrition and health behavior change communication program targeted to women in Burkina Faso reduces anemia, wasting, and diarrhea in children 3–12. 9 months of age at baseline: A cluster-randomized controlled trial. *Journal of Nutrition 145*, 1317–1324. https://doi.org/10.3945/jn.114.203539

Oxfam (2007). *Evaluation of sustainable livelihoods, internally displaced persons' (IDP) support, and emergency seed distribution projects in Eritrea.* Oxfam GB. https://seads-standards.org/wp-content/uploads/2021/04/OXFAM-2007-Eritrea.pdf

Richards, P. (2005, 29 June – 2 July). *The history and future of African rice: What we can learn from observing rice farming in West Africa war zones* [conference paper]. Africa-Europe Group for Interdisciplinary Studies conference, School of Oriental and Africa Studies, London.

Richards, P., Bah, K. & Vincent, J. (2004). *Social capital and survival: Prospects for community-driven development in post-conflict Sierra Leone.* Social development papers: community-driven development; conflict prevention and reconstruction series. Paper no. 12. World Bank. https://documents.worldbank.org/en/publication/documents-reports/documentdetail/685811468762926067/social-capital-and-survival-prospects-for-community-driven-development-in-post-conflict-sierra-leone

Ruel, M.T. & Alderman, H. (2013). Nutrition-sensitive interventions and programmes: How can they help to accelerate progress in improving maternal and child nutrition? *Lancet 382*, 536–551. https://doi.org/10.1016/S0140-6736(13)60843-0

Schreinemachers, P., Patalagsa, M.A. & Uddin, N. (2016). Impact and cost effectiveness of women's training in home gardening and nutrition in Bangladesh. *Journal of Development Effectiveness 8*, 473–488. https://doi.org/10.1080/19439342.2016.1231704

Sperling, L., Osborn T. & Cooper, D. (eds.) (2004). *Towards effective and sustainable seed relief activities.* Plant Production and Protection Paper #181. FAO. https://www.fao.org/3/y5703e/y5703e00.htm#Contents

Sperling, L., Remington, T. & Haugen, J. (2006). *Seed aid for seed security: Advice for practitioners.* Practice briefs 1–10. International Center for Tropical Agriculture and Catholic Relief Services. https://www.crs.org/sites/default/files/tools-research/seed-aid-for-seed-security.pdf

Walsh, S. & Sperling, L. (2019). *Review of practice and possibilities for market-led interventions in emergency seed security response.* International Center for Tropical Agriculture. https://hdl.handle.net/10568/108655

World Bank (2007). *From agriculture to nutrition: Pathways, synergies and outcomes.* World Bank. http://hdl.handle.net/10986/28183

Appendix 5.1: Initial assessment checklist for seed and seed system responses

These are suggested questions to ask when planning a seed or seed system response. The objective is to ensure that the minimum data are collected for assessment and response identification so that seed and seed system responses meet SEADS minimum standards. None of the questions is mandatory. Adapt the list to suit the context.

Background questions

1. What is the agriculture calendar?
2. What are the most important and preferred crops for food security, nutrition, and income in the main season and in any secondary seasons?
3. What are realistic sowing rates for main and secondary crops?
4. How much land does the average household plant per crop per season?
5. What gender dynamics exist in seed selection, knowledge transfer, sales, storage, and sowing?
6. How do formal and informal actors operate in the targeted area? What roles do crop producers play, and what roles do other actors play?
   a. Where do crop producers get seed?
   b. Who produces seed?
   c. Who improves seed?
   d. Where is seed stored?
   e. How is seed transported?
7. How do most crop producers get to markets to buy inputs or sell crops?
   a. What is the cost, if any, of that transportation?

Conclusion/exit

Do you understand the context of crop production and use of seed in normal times in the targeted area?

Crisis context

1. When in the agriculture calendar did the crisis occur?
2. Is land or soil available and safely accessible for crop production?
3. Do crop producers have access to productive assets and labor?
4. Are crop producers ready to engage in agriculture?

5. Can crops sown be reasonably expected to grow to maturity and be harvested in the current crisis context?
6. Are there any risks to specific vulnerable groups in their accessing markets at this time?
7. Do the risks of gender-based violence differ by response option? Does one response option pose fewer risks for women than another? How can gender-based violence risks of each possible option be mitigated?
8. Has the crisis affected preferred crops, sowing rates, production location and surface area, or formal and informal value-chain actors?

Conclusion/exit

Has an SSA been conducted, and what acute seed security constraints exist? If any, can they be appropriately addressed at this phase of the crisis? If the constraint is deemed acute:

a. Has seed and seed system support been provided in the target area for more than two seasons in a row in the past? If so, why?
b. Can the need continue to be considered acute?

Response identification and timing

1. Have people needing seed security-related assistance been adequately defined?
2. Is the response option acceptable to program participants? To crop producers?
3. If access to or provision of seed is selected:
   a. Does the drafted implementation timeline show consideration of oft-repeated bottlenecks and delivery of seed in time for the sowing season?
   b. Are there testing facilities? If no testing facilities are available, what alternative system can be used to assure seed quality?
   c. Is the seed quality on offer at least as good as producers routinely use and is the quality accepted by them?
   d. Is the quality also acceptable to donors, governments, and practitioners?
4. Do the objectives and proposed response strategy address the seed security constraint?
5. Is the required expertise and capacity in place to achieve the objectives (both within the lead institution and via collaborators)?
6. Have possible negative effects of the response been anticipated and necessary actions been programmed?
7. Is there time to implement the response before the targeted season?

Conclusion/exit

Can a proposed seed security response be completed in time for crop producers to have seed in hand for their normal planting period?

Appendix 5.2: Suggested seed quality indicators and targets

Table A5.1: Suggested seed quality indicators and targets

Attribute	Suggested indicators	Target
Physical	A minimum of damaged seed (broken, cracked, or shriveled)	Minimum 95–98% pure, as determined by analysis and dependent on the crop
Physiological	Germination rate: percentage of seed that can germinate and develop into normal seedlings	Minimum 70–80% depending on crop
	Seed vigor	Verified by crop producers and key informants
Genetic	Adapted to local soil types, soil fertility, diseases, pests, day length, moisture regimes	Verified by crop producers and key informants
	Suitable for local agronomic practices, such as manual or machine harvesting	Verified by crop producers
	Suitable for end use, including processing, cooking, and in terms of color and taste	Verified by end user
	Pest and disease tolerant	Verified by crop producers and key informants

| **Health** | A minimal number of diseased seeds, and absence of disease-causing organisms, such as fungi, bacteria, viruses, pests | Visual check: discoloration or staining on the seeds may indicate disease |

Modified from FAO (2010b)

CHAPTER 6:
TOOLS, EQUIPMENT, AND OTHER NON-SEED INPUTS

Minimum standards: tools, equipment, and other non-seed inputs

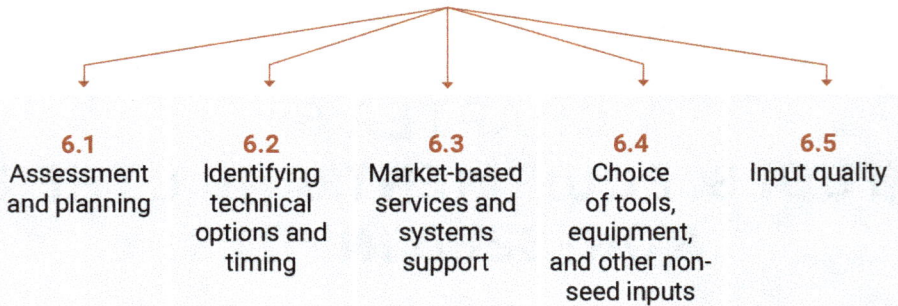

6.1
Assessment and planning

6.2
Identifying technical options and timing

6.3
Market-based services and systems support

6.4
Choice of tools, equipment, and other non-seed inputs

6.5
Input quality

CHAPTER 6: TOOLS, EQUIPMENT, AND OTHER NON-SEED INPUTS

> Annex A: Glossary contains definitions of some of the technical terms used in SEADS.

This chapter presents options for providing tools, equipment, and other non-seed inputs in a crop-related crisis response.

In a slow-onset crisis resulting from drought, pests (such as fall armyworm), and diseases (such as wheat rust), producers typically retain their tools and equipment and remain on their land. However, a multiyear drought or successive years of severe pest and disease infestations may result in the forced sale of production assets, such as livestock, tools, equipment, other non-seed inputs, and even land (AKLDP 2016). Where crop producers are affected by a crisis but retain access to their land, they can typically return to normal crop production within two to three years, through temporary sharecropping arrangements or diversifying their cropping to more resilient crops and varieties.

In contrast, the outcome of a rapid-onset or complex crisis may be mixed. For example, crop producers affected by flood, earthquake, volcanic eruption, typhoon, or conflict may not only lose production assets, but also be displaced from their land and homes. Whether displaced or not, such households may require support to be able to grow crops again. If they can integrate locally, return, or relocate safely, displaced crop producers may also require other forms of support to restore former cropping systems.

Links to the SEADS livelihood objectives

Providing tools, equipment, and other non-seed inputs relates to all three SEADS livelihood objectives:

1. to provide immediate livelihood benefits to crop-producing households affected by crisis.
2. to protect crop-related livelihoods of households affected by crisis.
3. to rebuild or support crop-related production, infrastructure, and systems to ensure livelihoods for households affected by crisis.

The livelihood benefits of tools, equipment, and other non-seed inputs can only be achieved if crops can be produced via grains (botanic seeds) or vegetative materials. See Chapter 5: Seed and Seed Systems to assess this pre-requisite to a tools, equipment, or non-seed input response.

If crop production is possible, and tools, equipment, and non-seed inputs (see Table 6.1) are available, accessible, and of suitable design and quality (see Table 6.2), crop production can be restored and protected after the crisis and continue in early recovery. This provides crop producers and their families with livelihood benefits of food and income (Objectives 1 and 2). Like seed and seed system responses, tools, equipment, and non-seed input responses can also improve preparedness and disaster risk reduction, protecting and strengthening crop production into the future (Objectives 2 and 3).

While the provision of tools, equipment, and other non-seed inputs may contribute to each of the SEADS livelihood objectives, it may not be adequate to meet all crop producers' needs. This is because most small-scale crop producers are net consumers who depend on diversified livelihoods (Woodhill et al. 2020).

The importance of providing tools, equipment, and other non-seed inputs in crisis response

Access to appropriate tools, equipment, and other non-seed inputs is critical for crop production. Tools and equipment enable land preparation, planting, weeding, harvesting, and storage. Soil amendments, including organic and inorganic chemicals, nurture soil health, protect growing crops, and increase yields. Cash transfers and access to credit support the seasonal hire of labor and machinery (Sustainable Food Lab 2016). Without such inputs and the systems that support them, crop producers would be unable to produce crops, hunger and poverty would increase, and longer-term sustainable livelihoods would be put at risk.

Table 6.1 gives examples of the tools, equipment, and other non-seed inputs that are typically provided in a crop-related crisis response.

Table 6.1: Crop producers need a range of tools, equipment, and other non-seed inputs to support their livelihoods

Tools	Equipment	Other non-seed inputs
<ul><li>Hand hoes</li><li>Slashers</li><li>Sharpening stones</li><li>Watering cans</li><li>Corn huskers</li><li>Winnowing sieves</li></ul>	<ul><li>Work boots</li><li>Protective clothing (for handling chemicals)</li><li>Crop storage sacks or bins</li><li>Replacement water pumps, grinding mills, and oil expellers</li><li>Temporary fencing materials, including posts, rails, wire netting, nails, and staples</li></ul>	<ul><li>Topsoil</li><li>Sacks (for sack gardens)</li><li>Stones for building terrace and keyhole gardens</li><li>Soil amendments (ash, mulch, compost, and lime)</li><li>Organic and inorganic fertilizer</li><li>Organic and inorganic pesticides</li><li>Cash and credit for the hire of seasonal labor, machinery, and purchase of fuel for equipment</li></ul>

Providing tools, equipment, and non-seed inputs overcomes four potential constraints, described in Table 6.2. These constraints mirror those in Table 5.1.

Table 6.2: Four types of constraints typically affect crop producers affected by a crisis

Constraint	Characteristics required to overcome the constraint
Availability	An adequate quantity of appropriate tools, equipment, and other non-seed inputs is available in the area (spatial availability), at the right time to support seasonal cropping activity (temporal availability), including land preparation, sowing, weeding, protection, and harvesting
Access	Crop producers and others interested in growing crops for the first time acquire the tools, equipment, and other non-seed inputs they need without: • economic barriers to purchase or barter • physical barriers, including distance to market, security threats, and quarantine restrictions • sociocultural barriers (disability, age, gender, ethnicity, and other biases), language gaps, and difficulty accessing information
Quality	Tools, equipment, and other non-seed inputs are adapted to local crop production systems and have desired and appropriate local traits. See Minimum Standard 6.5 for details
Design suitability	Tools and equipment meet different crop producers' (men, women, and children) preferences

In addition to supporting the intended recipient, responses also benefit wholesalers, sellers, and other value-chain actors, as recipient households may seek the services of local blacksmiths and agricultural engineers for the maintenance, repair, and eventual replacement of tools and equipment. Tools and equipment may also be used for other livelihood needs, such as to construct and improve housing and livestock shelters. They can be shared between different households, including those of internally displaced people and refugees, affected by a crisis (Cullis 2020, Pajot 2020).

Finally, there is increasing evidence that growing food and flowers improves self-esteem and mental health (Millican et al. 2019, RHS 2021) and builds resilience (Cullis 2020). Recognizing these additional benefits, an increasing number of humanitarian actors are providing the necessary tools, equipment, and other non-seed inputs for households affected by crisis to grow crops for food and to grow flowers.

Technical options for supporting tools, equipment, and other non-seed inputs

This chapter presents three technical options and several sub-options for providing tools, equipment, and other non-seed inputs in a crisis:

- facilitate access to inputs
- provide inputs
- support formal and informal input systems.

Wherever possible, prefer facilitated access over direct distribution, as the latter should only be used where markets are not working. Support for formal and informal systems can, over time, strengthen input systems affected by disasters and support a transition from direct distribution. It may be appropriate to support different options for different user groups even in the same community. For example, some households may benefit from commodity vouchers for tools, equipment, or fuel for an irrigation pump. Others, who need to plant on poorer land, may benefit from compost distribution, while others may benefit from support to local blacksmiths for improved lightweight tools.

These three technical options were selected based on available evidence of impact from agriculture responses in humanitarian crisis (SEADS 2021) and on expert opinion. However, evidence did not disaggregate what caused the impact on livelihoods when a combination of response areas and technical options was used to address all identified constraints.

Evidence indicates that combinations of response areas and technical options can lead to crop productivity increases and improve livelihood outcomes, either through increased food security, reduced food expenditures, or increased income. See for example, Mollet 2009, FAO 2012a, FAO 2012b, World Bank 2012, Pretari & Anguko 2019, and Cullis 2020 in the *SEADS Evidence Database*. As such, the technical options and guidance in this chapter can also be used when providing household kits for community-led infrastructure rehabilitation covered in Chapter 7: Crop-related Infrastructure.

Case Study 5.1 (see SEADS website) provides an example of seed and tool provision resulting in extra months of food self-sufficiency.

Technical Option 1: Facilitate access

Facilitated access to tools, equipment, and other non-seed inputs includes any action that reduces economic, physical, or sociocultural barriers to access. As a result, crop producers can again prepare their land, plant, weed, nurture, protect, and harvest increased yields.

Importantly, a market-based response (see SEADS Principle 1: Use livelihoods-based programming) to facilitating access to tools, equipment, and other non-seed inputs can restore crop production while supporting local sellers and markets (see *MERS*). Table 6.3 lists various market-based sub-options and the access barriers that they address.

Table 6.3: Several sub-options are available to facilitate access to tools, equipment, and non-seed inputs

Technical sub-options	Barriers addressed		
	Economic	Physical	Sociocultural
1.1. Cash support for producers to purchase tools, equipment, and other non-seed inputs available in local markets	x		
1.2. Cash support for blacksmiths, agricultural engineers, and sellers to reach disaster-affected areas	x		
1.3. Transport subsidies for sellers to transport inputs to markets close to targeted crop producers		x	x
1.4. Grants to input sellers to supply internally displaced people's camps		x	x
1.5. Grant support for input fairs	x	x	x

Case Study 6.1 (see SEADS website) illustrates an innovative unconditional cash cost-share arrangement.

Technical Option 2: Provide inputs

Where tools, equipment, and other non-seed inputs are unavailable, including in remote, inaccessible, and insecure areas where markets are non-functional, it may be necessary to procure, transport, and directly distribute inputs to crop producers affected by crisis.

Humanitarian actors may distribute these inputs, or they may seek the support of local stakeholders, such as producer cooperatives and women's groups, to undertake distributions. Engaging local stakeholders not only builds local capacity, but also may help reduce operational delays that often characterize large-scale government and humanitarian responses. See SEADS Principle 2: Use a participatory approach in all aspects of crisis response for more guidance on including local stakeholders in assessment, design, and implementation.

Case Study 6.2 (see SEADS website) illustrates how direct distribution of fertilizer and hand tools resulted in production above self-sufficiency levels in an area where a typhoon had destroyed irrigated rice, coconut, and other crops.

Technical Option 3: Support to formal and informal input systems

In normal times, service providers and systems provide access to tools, equipment, and other non-seed inputs for crop producers. Crises may weaken or temporarily end such service provision. They are, however, seldom destroyed, except in a long-term complex crisis. Where this has happened, support in the form of grants and loans can help rebuild services and systems. The process of rebuilding is often complex, takes several years, and may require a mixture of public and private investment.

Support for service and systems strengthening should be balanced across a range of providers throughout the different stages of the production cycle (land preparation, improving soil health, crop production, harvesting, and storage). Grants and credit schemes, technical and skills training for tool and equipment makers, and support for research and development of adapted tools, equipment, and non-seed inputs are examples of support to formal and informal systems.

Advantages and disadvantages of each technical option

The advantages and disadvantages of each technical option for providing tools, equipment, and non-seed inputs are summarized in Table 6.4.

Table 6.4: Each tools, equipment, and other non-seed inputs option has advantages and disadvantages

Option	Advantages	Disadvantages
1. Facilitate access to inputs	• The use of cash and vouchers improves timely delivery • Supports crop producers' priorities and choices • Cash injections strengthen the local economy through the multiplier effect • Delivery is flexible, including through mobile phones, electronic vouchers, cards (for example, pre-paid, ATM, smart, credit, or debit cards), or cash distributions • Support can be tailored to the different needs of men, women, children, and marginalized groups • Tools, equipment, and non-seed input choices can be monitored and inform the design of future programs	• Cash distributions may not be fully used for the planned procurement of tools, equipment, and other non-seed inputs, as households affected by a crisis typically face a range of competing priorities, including food, health, and education • Local input fairs require considerable organization, may delay access to critical inputs, reach relatively small numbers, and be inappropriate in areas affected by conflict • To meet quantity or quality requirements, voucher schemes may not equitably benefit small-scale input sellers, who cannot provide storage or

		transportation or simply because it is logistically challenging to contract with a diversity of vendors
2. Provide inputs	• Distributions can target and reach remote areas that are poorly serviced by markets • Familiar to humanitarian actors and crop producers facing recurrent crises • Process and assistance can be standardized across contexts • Possible to reach large numbers of crisis-affected crop producers • Quality issues can be relatively easily controlled through spot checks • Simplicity of monitoring, including the number and range of tools, equipment, and other non-seed inputs delivered and the number of recipients	• Standard packages may not meet the needs and priorities of different groups (men, women, children, and marginalized and minority groups) or be appropriate for different crop production systems • Large-scale responses favor large-scale operations at the expense of small-scale, local input sellers • Procurement and logistical challenges, including availability of storage warehouses, that may result in delayed distributions and failure to meet livelihood objectives • Direct distributions can become the norm and undermine local formal and informal markets, including those recovering from crisis • Large-scale direct distributions can disrupt systems,

...continued

		reduce diversity and choice, create dependency, and stifle innovation
3. Support to formal and informal input systems	• Support can be tailored to the needs of blacksmiths, agricultural engineers, and agriculture supply stores, including those displaced by a crisis • Support can improve the design of tools and equipment to meet the needs of different user groups (men, women, and different age groups) • Support has a potential multiplier effect in the local economy • Support can be tailored to build relations between local input sellers and affected crop producers	• Support can result in the development of designs and products that have little or no sustained market value • Subsidies can support inefficient small business enterprises that are not competitive in normal times

Timing of tools, equipment, and other non-seed input technical options

Crop production crisis responses typically take place after essential lifesaving responses are managed. Use local agriculture calendars to ensure timely support. FAO's *Crop Calendar Information Tool* provides online versions of local calendars (2021). Table 6.5 presents example timelines for implementing the three technical options across a generic agriculture calendar for maize and beans.

Table 6.5: Timing of tools, equipment, and other non-seed inputs technical options to coincide with local cropping seasons—example of maize and beans production

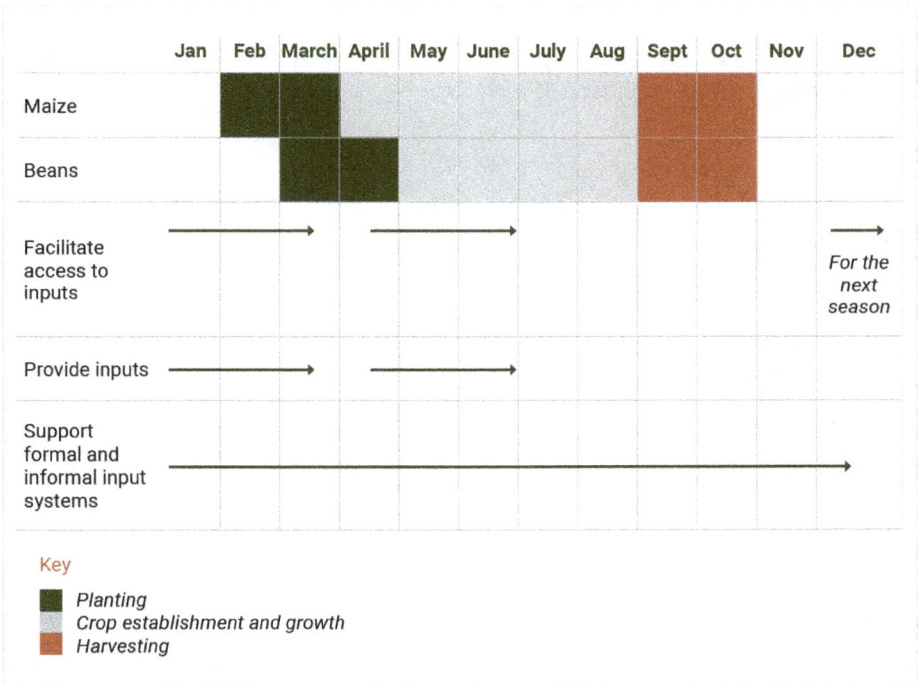

	Jan	Feb	March	April	May	June	July	Aug	Sept	Oct	Nov	Dec
Maize		Planting	Planting	Crop establishment and growth	Crop establishment and growth	Crop establishment and growth	Crop establishment and growth	Crop establishment and growth	Harvesting	Harvesting		
Beans			Planting	Planting	Crop establishment and growth	Crop establishment and growth	Crop establishment and growth	Crop establishment and growth	Harvesting			
Facilitate access to inputs	←———→			←————→								←→ *For the next season*
Provide inputs	←———→			←————→								
Support formal and informal input systems	←——————————————————————————————————————→											

Key

■ *Planting*
▨ *Crop establishment and growth*
■ *Harvesting*

The provision of tools, equipment, and other non-seed inputs is time sensitive, as delays can affect crop growth, health, and yield and because crop producers need to plan and organize required labor ahead of time. If, due to lack of confidence in a planned input response, they feel unable to plan and organize labor, they may move scarce labor resources to other economic and livelihood activities, and opportunities are lost.

The phase of the crisis also informs response timing for tools, equipment, and non-seed inputs, as Table 6.6 shows.

For example, in the immediate aftermath of a rapid-onset or complex crisis, priority is rightly given to lifesaving responses, so support for tools, equipment, and other non-seed inputs should be delayed until basic needs are met.

The response for a slow-onset crisis, such as those caused by drought, pests, or disease, is different. For multiyear droughts, organizations are often already operational, so providing tools, equipment, and other non-seed inputs ahead of the next growing season should not pose significant challenges. However, providing such inputs would be inappropriate during the crisis itself and during the recovery phase.

Table 6.6: Different tools, equipment, and other non-seed input technical options are relevant at different phases of a crisis

TECHNICAL OPTIONS	Emergency phase	Recovery phase
Rapid-onset and complex crisis		
Facilitate access to inputs	⟶	
Provide inputs	⟶	
Support formal and informal input systems	————————————————⟶	
Slow-onset crisis		
Facilitate access to inputs	⟶	
Provide inputs	⟶	
Support formal and informal input systems	————————————————⟶	

Before committing to a response, whether in a rapid-onset, slow-onset, or complex crisis, consult national and international meteorological services. If normal conditions are expected, then the response can go ahead. If, however, the forecast is for poor rains, it may be better to delay the response and wait until the next forecast for good rains.

State and non-state actors can support and strengthen services and systems for providing tools, equipment, and other non-seed inputs in all phases of a crisis as long as they do not interfere with the provision of basic needs.

Decision tree to select technical options

A decision tree can guide your choice of technical options. It prompts you to consider the variables in a systematic way. Decision tree questions are ordered in terms of priority to program quality.

Answer Question 1 first (either "yes" or "no"). The decision tree directs you to a new question based on your answer. "No" responses indicate that other suitable responses identified in the response-area identification tool (RAIT) should be considered or that further training or capacity building may be required to answer "yes" to the questions. As multiple technical options may be appropriate, when one technical option has been selected the decision tree will lead you to consideration of others.

Your answers should be based on all data at your disposal, but in particular:

- the results of the initial assessment (see Chapter 4: Assessment for Crop-related Crisis Response)
- a theory of change (see Minimum Standard 8.2: Project objectives)
- your organization's capacity to achieve relevant minimum standards in this chapter (see Annex B).

SEADS recommends that you use a RAIT (see Minimum Standard 4.4: Selecting response areas) before completing a decision tree. The RAIT will indicate whether tools, equipment, and other non-seed inputs responses are necessary, appropriate, and feasible, and which livelihood objective they may have the greatest impact on.

Use Figure 6.1 to test whether tools, equipment, and other non-seed inputs should be part of a crop-related response and, if so, which technical options will be most appropriate.

Tools, equipment, and other non-seed inputs minimum standards

Minimum Standard 6.1: Assessment and planning

Assessments are conducted to determine the level of interest in returning to crop production; the need for tools, equipment, and other non-seed inputs; and the functionality of local market-based services and systems.

Key actions

- Carry out initial assessment using participatory approaches to understand the demand for tools, equipment, and non-seed inputs (see Guidance note 1).
- Ensure staff have relevant technical competencies to understand and utilize key information (see Guidance note 2).

Figure 6.1: Decision tree for tools, equipment, and other non-seed inputs

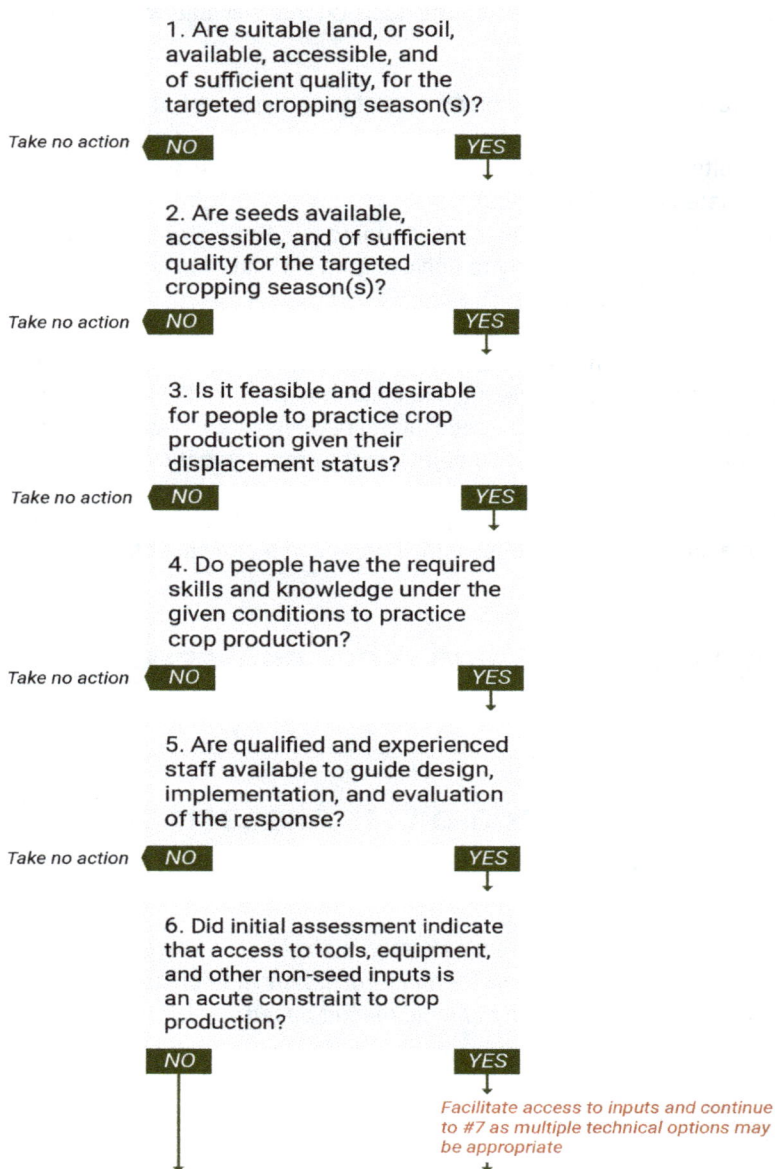

1. Are suitable land, or soil, available, accessible, and of sufficient quality, for the targeted cropping season(s)?

Take no action ← **NO**   **YES** ↓

2. Are seeds available, accessible, and of sufficient quality for the targeted cropping season(s)?

Take no action ← **NO**   **YES** ↓

3. Is it feasible and desirable for people to practice crop production given their displacement status?

Take no action ← **NO**   **YES** ↓

4. Do people have the required skills and knowledge under the given conditions to practice crop production?

Take no action ← **NO**   **YES** ↓

5. Are qualified and experienced staff available to guide design, implementation, and evaluation of the response?

Take no action ← **NO**   **YES** ↓

6. Did initial assessment indicate that access to tools, equipment, and other non-seed inputs is an acute constraint to crop production?

NO   **YES** ↓

Facilitate access to inputs and continue to #7 as multiple technical options may be appropriate ↓

(Continued on next page)

7. Did initial assessment indicate that availability of tools, equipment, and other non-seed inputs is an acute constraint to crop production?

NO   YES

Provide inputs and continue to #8 as multiple technical options may be appropriate

8. Did initial assessment indicate that support to value-chain actors could reduce the acute availability constraint in the targeted cropping season(s)?

NO   YES   *Support formal and informal input systems*

9. Did initial assessment indicate that quality or design suitability of tools, equipment, and other non-seed inputs is an acute constraint to crop production?

Take no action   NO   YES   *Support formal and informal input systems*

Note: The result *Take no action* does not necessarily mean that no response should take place, but rather that other suitable responses identified in the RAIT should be considered or further training or capacity building may be required to answer "yes" to the questions. Where no other suitable options exist and training and capacity building is not possible, support to alternative livelihoods can be considered.

- Use Appendix 4.1: Example questions to gather initial and technical data and Appendix 6.1: Initial assessment checklist for tools, equipment, and other non-seed input responses to select assessment questions.

- Understand acute availability, access, quality, and design quality constraints that impact tools, equipment, and non-seed inputs used for cropping (see Guidance note 3).

- Link long-standing chronic input needs with development programs (see Guidance note 4).

Guidance notes

1.   Initial assessment. The crisis may have resulted in new and different livelihood aspirations (especially when people are displaced), as hunger is no guarantee of continued interest in or commitment to growing crops. An initial assessment can identify changed expectations or need for tools, equipment, or non-seed inputs (see SEADS Principle 1, SEADS Principle 2, and Chapter 4). Appendix 6.1 includes questions that can be used to assess whether a tools, equipment, and non-seed inputs response will have livelihood benefits.

It is important to assess the needs of different groups, including women, different age groups, and persons with disabilities, and not necessarily expect them to use tools and equipment designed for men (Cronin 2020). Facilitating cooperation between different user groups and local input service and systems providers may result in the production of lightweight or specially adapted tools and equipment. Adapted tools and equipment enable different groups to work more effectively and typically result in less damage to growing crops. In the same way, different crop producers may have different levels of interest in accessing soil amendments, organic and inorganic pesticides and fertilizers, and grants and credit to hire seasonal labor or machinery, or purchase fuel to run irrigation pumps.

Case Study 6.3 (see SEADS website) describes how an imported combine harvester was adapted to fit local needs.

2.   Team competencies. An effective response will depend on an understanding of the frequency of use of tools, equipment, and non-seed inputs in normal times. It also requires an understanding of the services and systems that underpin them, including local blacksmiths and agricultural engineers, and that needs vary across different population groups. Annex B provides guidance on the desired and essential elements of team competencies for design, implementation, and evaluation of crop-related responses. Without these skill sets, key contextual information can be overlooked and the design of planned assistance can be flawed.

3.   Tailored support. Crop producers seldom have the same amount of land, work the same soils, choose the same crops, have access to the same amount of labor, or use identical non-seed inputs. The same is true for displaced households. Some may accept access to one or two relatively small containers in which to establish a small kitchen garden. Others may want to rent plots and fields from host community members. Other people in the same camp setting may have little or no experience in growing crops, while others may be displaced blacksmiths, agricultural engineers, and input sellers. Service providers may be more interested in re-establishing themselves in their former trades than growing crops. Finally, some displaced individuals, including those suffering trauma, may be more interested in growing flowers than crops.

Tailoring tools, equipment, and other non-seed input support to the needs and interests of different households can meet diverse needs and ensure that inputs are used and value for money is achieved.

Case Study 6.4 (see SEADS website) describes how refugee households increased food availability, access, and sales following distribution of a tailored bundle of seeds, tools, soil amendments, training, and fencing materials. The questions in Appendix 6.1 can help to determine those specific needs.

4. **Acute versus chronic constraints.** Assessment can help differentiate between acute and chronic needs (see Appendix 4.1). Crisis responses are not well suited to address chronic unmet tools, equipment, or non-seed input needs, which are better resolved through longer-term poverty reduction and development programs.

Minimum Standard 6.2: Identifying technical options and timing

Appropriate tools, equipment, and other non-seed inputs are delivered in time for the growing season.

Key actions

- Use the decision tree in Figure 6.1 to select appropriate technical options for the type of crisis and the agriculture calendar. The options identified should promote social equity (see Guidance note 1).

- Estimate response costs based on appropriate targeting, real-time costs, and appropriate and safe delivery mechanism(s) (see Guidance notes 2 and 3).

- Devise a timeline for the identified response and assess and address potential bottlenecks that might delay delivery (see Guidance note 4).

- Identify and reduce protection risks that might arise from the identified response (see Guidance note 5).

Guidance notes

1.   **Participatory approaches and social equity.** SEADS Principle 2 and Chapter 4 provide more detail on participatory approaches and emphasize the importance of inclusive participation. Confirm the appropriateness of the technical option(s) selected, considering whether longer-term development assistance is available to planned recipients.

2.   **Scale of assistance.** Having identified potential technical options, the next step is to calculate the cost and tailor the scale of assistance, in terms of the cost per recipient (depth of response) and the number of recipients (breadth of response). To do this, consider the full costs of the response, including procurement, transport, and operational support. Operational costs in crisis contexts may fluctuate and be inflated. The *MERS* Asset Distribution Standard 1 provides useful guidance.

3.   **Targeting.** Design a real-time participatory approach to targeting based on a comprehensive understanding of social and cultural norms. Community-based targeting typically provides a more effective means of ensuring the appropriate and full distribution of assistance to all vulnerable groups (see SEADS Principle 2).

4.   **Delivery bottlenecks.** Delays in delivering tools, equipment, and non-seed inputs can result in a failure to meet livelihood objectives. Such delays are particularly problematic when tools for land preparation are involved and a cropping season is put at risk. Delays are common in areas of conflict and remote locations where roads are poor and the cost of transport higher, so it helps to anticipate and plan for them.

5.   **Do no harm.** A crisis, particularly a complex crisis that is compounded by conflict and violence, typically results in theft, looting, coercion, exploitation, deprivation, and sexual violence. For people recovering from trauma, it is important that the delivery of tools, equipment, and non-seed inputs does not put them at further risk and that participatory decision making ensures appropriate delivery systems (see the Protection Principles in the *Sphere Handbook*).

Minimum Standard 6.3: Market-based services and systems support

Preference is given to the provision of appropriate tools, equipment, and other non-seed inputs through market-based services and systems.

Key actions

- Use livelihoods-based programming to inform delivery options (see Guidance notes 1 and 2).

- Ensure responses foster vibrant local services and systems that ensure longer-term choice of tools, equipment, and other non-seed inputs (see Guidance note 3).

- Use specialist advisory support for the design of responses (see Guidance note 4).

Guidance notes

1. **Livelihoods-based approach.** Use a livelihoods approach to consider all aspects of the cropping system, including availability of and access to land through the entire cropping season, soil health, access to appropriate tools, equipment, and other non-seed inputs, and existing market-based services and systems (see SEADS Principle 1). The *Emergency Market Mapping and Analysis Toolkit* (Albu 2010) can help highlight strengths and weaknesses in tools, equipment, and other non-seed input markets, services, and systems.

2. **Market choice.** Crop producers are familiar with markets, and many routinely attend weekly local markets. Those who do are typically comfortable with selecting tools, equipment, and other non-seed inputs. The appropriateness of a market-based delivery mechanism depends on factors such as availability of household labor, cash, and credit. The wider the choice, the more likely markets are to have a positive impact on livelihoods.

3. **Local versus external service and systems strengthening.** Experience suggests that cash-based responses can be biased towards larger tools,

equipment, and non-seed input companies over local blacksmiths, agricultural engineers, and agriculture supply stores, who cannot achieve required levels of scale. Direct distributions particularly benefit external value-chain actors and do not support local services and systems. Where it is not possible to use local value-chain actors to facilitate access or directly distribute tools, equipment, and non-seed inputs, it may be possible to support them through grants, improved access to credit, and support for research and innovation.

4. Humanitarian bundling. Tools, equipment, and other non-seed inputs are typically a component of a larger bundle of humanitarian assistance that might include cash and/or food assistance, shelter, other non-food items, and seeds. Where distributed with other assistance, involving specialists (such as crop specialists and agricultural engineers familiar with crisis contexts) in the design of non-seed inputs responses results in improved outcomes. See Annex B for desired and essential competencies.

Case Study 6.5 (see SEADS website) describes how agriculture specialists working on longer-term projects in the region developed a responsive package of assistance that supported internally displaced people to produce food and make impressive food security gains.

Minimum Standard 6.4: Choice of tools, equipment, and other non-seed inputs

Tools, equipment, and other non-seed inputs are appropriate for local agro-ecological conditions and adapted for different users.

Key actions

- Ensure that tools, equipment, and other non-seed inputs are tailored to the needs of households with different labor availability and capacities (see Guidance notes 1 and 2).
- Confirm donor and host government acceptability of selected tools, equipment, and other non-seed inputs (see Guidance note 3).
- Carefully consider the benefits of introducing new tools, equipment, and other non-seed inputs in a crop-related crisis response (see Guidance note 4).

- Assess the need for training to ensure the appropriate use of inputs (see Guidance note 5).

Guidance notes

1. **Livelihood objectives.** Tailor tools, equipment, and other non-seed inputs to meet the SEADS livelihood objectives (see Table 2.1 and SEADS Principle 1). This might result in the delivery of different packages for men, women, different age groups, and marginalized groups. For example, one package might be tailored to support early benefits and another to support the longer-term rebuilding of cropping systems affected by the crisis. Providing hand tools for land preparation and planting, or providing cash for fuel for an irrigation pump to support a standing crop, is more time sensitive than providing compost or other amendments that build soil health over time.

2. **Household preferences.** Households recovering from a rapid-onset or complex crisis may choose to plant different crops and varieties than they did before the crisis. Their needs for tools and equipment may similarly change. Confirming current needs and priorities of different households, including the needs and priorities of women, child-headed, and marginalized families, is therefore important (see the Protection Principles in the *Sphere Handbook* and SEADS Principle 2). Consider the weight of tools, as those that are too heavy for the user typically result in handling injuries and damage to growing crops.

3. **Context acceptability.** Different donors and host governments may have different requirements, restrictions, and regulations to govern the use of organic and inorganic amendments, fertilizers, and pesticides. The initial assessment can include aspects of acceptability and support adaptation to different restrictions and regulations and ensure input package acceptability. It may be necessary to distribute packages of tools, equipment, and other non-seed inputs—including fuel for irrigation pumps—in several rounds so key inputs are available on time. For equipment that can be temporary or permanent, consider factors such as how long targeted participants will be in the crop production location or whether temporary equipment can be modified later to become more permanent. Chapter 7 provides guidance on permanent infrastructure and Chapter 8 of the *Livestock Emergency Guidelines and Standards* on livestock shelter and settlement includes considerations for deciding on temporary or permanent infrastructure.

4. **Traditional versus modern.** Crop producers typically have strong preferences for tools, equipment, and other non-seed inputs, shaped by years of experience.

Ensuring that tools of choice are available, including traditional designs, is important. This may be particularly important for people that have suffered trauma, as familiar inputs may have mental health benefits. In other cases, working with women, children, and marginalized groups to improve the design of tools and equipment may result in the production of improved, lightweight tools that are more appropriate for them. Supporting increased choice may help more households achieve SEADS Livelihood Objective 1. Likewise, consider providing choice when replacing wear parts of irrigation pumps to assess the possibility of upgrades and green technology. Note that wear parts of irrigation pumps may be part of permanent infrastructure that needs rehabilitation, which is covered in Chapter 7.

5. **Training and capacity building.** Design training and capacity-building support to fill essential knowledge gaps, including the appropriate and safe use of soil amendments, fertilizers, and pesticides (both organic and inorganic). Tailor all training and capacity building to the needs and interests of different groups (men, women, children, and marginalized groups) using participatory training techniques. Local sellers and extension services can provide useful guidance and support, including appropriate handling of agro-chemicals (see SEADS Principle 4: Selecting response areas).

Minimum Standard 6.5: Input quality

Tools, equipment, and other non-seed input responses meet the minimum quality required by crop-producing communities, practitioners, and donor organizations.

Key actions

- Confirm the quality of the tools, equipment, and other non-seed inputs are at least as good as crop producers are routinely used to and therefore are acceptable (see Guidance notes 1 and 2).
- Allow adequate time to check tools, equipment, and other non-seed inputs at the point of distribution, and be prepared to reject bad-quality inputs (see Guidance note 2).

- Ensure that all chemicals are properly labeled in the local language (see Guidance note 3).

Guidance notes

1. **Aspects of quality.** Tools, equipment, and other non-seed inputs should perform at or above anticipated levels and be sufficiently durable to ensure a long service life with normal use. In the same way that quality tools, equipment, and other non-seed inputs can have a positive impact on livelihoods, poor-quality inputs threaten impacts. Breakages may result in personal injury. The initial assessment and technical analyses should therefore establish quality criteria and screen out sellers who do not meet them.

Equally important quality issues are associated with the distribution of other non-seed inputs, such as topsoil, soil amendments, fertilizers, and pesticides. Topsoil should be as described, and not poorer-quality sub-soil, and soil amendments need to be of high quality to enrich poor soil and build soil health. Fertilizers and pesticides also need to be of high quality, not exceeding the expiration date or stored in poor conditions. Do not distribute fertilizers and pesticides that do not meet agreed quality criteria.

2. **Quality checking.** Planning a small number of spot checks at procurement, distribution, and periodically through the life of the response can address quality issues and also maintenance, repair, and replacement needs.

3. **Labeling.** Whether organic or inorganic, fertilizers and pesticides should be clearly labeled, including guidance on recommended application rates and safe use. Labeling should be in the local language and be clear in written and pictorial form, so everyone in the community can learn how to protect themselves and the environment.

Recommended reading

Details of references cited in this chapter are in Annex C. Further recommended reading includes:

Boedeker, W., Watts, M., Clausing, P. & Marquez, E. (2020). The global distribution of acute unintentional pesticide poisoning: Estimations based on a systematic review. *BMC Public Health 20.* https://bmcpublichealth.biomedcentral.com/articles/10.1186/s12889-020-09939-0

Food and Agriculture Organization (FAO) (2021, 12 May). *Q&A on pests and pesticide management.* FAO. http://www.fao.org/news/story/en/item/1398779/icode/

FAO & World Health Organization (2016). *International code of conduct on pesticide management: Guidelines on highly hazardous pesticides.* FAO & WHO. https://www.fao.org/pest-and-pesticide-management/pesticide-risk-reduction/hhps/en/

Gerard, B., Baudron, F. & Yahaya, R. (2019). Debunking myths about agricultural labor and mechanization in Africa: Fact sheet. International Maize and Wheat Improvement Center (CIMMYT) https://repository.cimmyt.org/handle/10883/20122

Gill, H.K. & Garg, H. (2019). Pesticides: Environmental impacts and management strategies. In M.L. Larramendy & S. Soloneski (eds.), *Pesticides* (Chapter 8). IntechOpen. https://www.intechopen.com/chapters/46083

Gummert, M. (2019). *Post-harvest technologies for small farmers.* International Rice Research Institute (IRRI). https://flar.org/wp-content/uploads/2019/01/009_Post-harvest-technologies-foe-small-farmers_MGummert.pdf

IRRI (2022). *Rice knowledge bank* [website]. http://www.knowledgebank.irri.org/

Maulu, S., Hasimuna, O. J., Mutale, B., Mphande, J. & Siankwilimba, E. (2021). Enhancing the role of rural agricultural extension programs in poverty alleviation: a review. *Cogent Food & Agriculture 7.* https://doi.org/10.1080/23311932.2021.1886663

Mock, N. & Vallet, M. (2018). *Review of food for peace market-based emergency food assistance programs – Sierra Leone case study report.* TANGO International. https://www.calpnetwork.org/wp-content/uploads/2020/03/pa00t2c4-1.pdf

Sims, B. & Kienzle, J. (2006). *Farm power and mechanization for small farms in sub-Saharan Africa*. FAO. https://www.fao.org/publications/card/en/c/6e76ecd0-1097-588c-ab99-7c5d29a6d055/

Sims, B., Kahan, D., Mpagalile, J., Hilmi, M. & Valle, S.S. (2018). *Hire services as a business enterprise: A training manual for small-scale mechanization service providers*. FAO. http://www.fao.org/family-farming/detail/en/c/1166249/

Sphere (2019). *Reducing environmental impact in humanitarian response*. Sphere Thematic Sheet 1. https://spherestandards.org/wp-content/uploads/Sphere-thematic-sheet-environment-EN.pdf

United Nations Office for Disaster Risk Reduction (UNDRR) (2021). *Global risk assessment framework (GRAF)* [webpage]. https://www.preventionweb.net/understanding-disaster-risk/graf

Appendix 6.1: Initial assessment checklist for tools, equipment, and other non-seed input responses

These are suggested questions to ask when planning a tools, equipment, and other non-seed input response. The objective is to ensure that the minimum data are collected for assessment and response identification so that the tools, equipment, and other non-seed input response meets the SEADS minimum standards. None of the questions is mandatory. Adapt the list to suit the context.

Context

1. What key tools, equipment, and other non-seed inputs for each of the primary and secondary crops do different households require, from land preparation to harvesting (according to wealth, and men/women/child-headed households)?
2. What are the normal market service providers and systems that make tools, equipment, and other non-seed inputs available?
   a. Who produces them?
   b. Where are they produced?
   c. How are they transported?
   d. Who is involved in the transport and sale at each stage?
   e. How accessible are they to different wealth groups and men/women/children?

Crisis context

1. What are the main tools, equipment, and other non-seed input constraints to producing crops safely?
2. What tools, equipment, and other non-seed inputs are most needed to ensure that affected crop producers can produce preferred crops through to harvest?
3. Are these tools, equipment, and other non-seed inputs available in local markets, and are there any risks to specific groups in accessing markets?
4. Do any of the response options result in increased risks for any group (men, women, children, marginalized groups)? How can risks be mitigated?

Response identification and timing

1. Have those people who need tools, equipment, and other non-seed inputs been adequately defined? Have the needs of men, women, children, and marginalized groups been defined?
2. Is the planned response option acceptable to the recipients including men/women and children and other marginalized groups?
3. If access to or provision of tools, equipment, and other non-seed inputs is selected:
   a. Do the draft implementation timelines address bottlenecks and ensure delivery of tools, equipment, and other non-seed inputs in time for the sowing season?
   b. Are the tools, equipment, and other non-seed inputs of similar quality to inputs that are routinely used and accepted?
   c. Is the quality also acceptable to donors, governments, and practitioners?
4. Do the objectives and proposed response strategy address the tools, equipment, and other non-seed input constraint(s)?
5. Does the lead implementing institution have the required livelihoods, market, and technical expertise and capacity to achieve SEADS livelihood objectives?
6. Have possible unintended impacts and the necessary adjustments been considered?

CHAPTER 7: CROP-RELATED INFRASTRUCTURE

Minimum standards: crop-related infrastructure

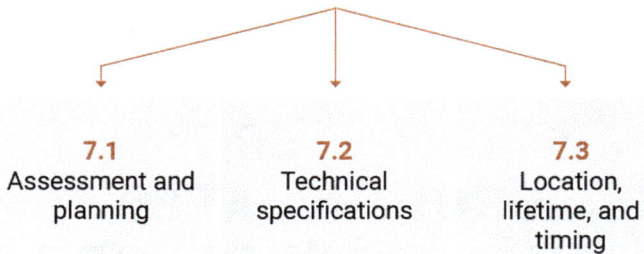

7.1
Assessment and planning

7.2
Technical specifications

7.3
Location, lifetime, and timing

CHAPTER 7: CROP-RELATED INFRASTRUCTURE

> Annex A: Glossary contains definitions of some of the technical terms used in SEADS.

This chapter provides options for rehabilitation of crop-related infrastructure. *Rehabilitation* includes the repair, rebuilding, replacement, or protection of temporary or permanent crop-related infrastructure used by individual households or groups of households in a community. *Crop-related infrastructure* includes buildings and property used for the production, transport, storage, and marketing of crops. Examples include greenhouses, shades, irrigation works, ponds, dams, roads, bridges, fencing, market stalls, silos, and warehouses.

Different types of crisis affect crop-related infrastructure in different ways:

- A rapid-onset crisis, such as floods, earthquakes, and typhoons, can damage or destroy infrastructure, preventing users from continuing their livelihood activities.
- A complex crisis can affect infrastructure in a similar way to a rapid-onset crisis, but multiple issues happen simultaneously. If conventional war is an element of a complex crisis, crop-related infrastructure may become unusable due to direct damage and remnants of war, such as landmines and unexploded ordnance.
- A slow-onset crisis, such as drought, can lead to the accumulation of dust, silt, and debris, which causes irrigation infrastructure malfunction when the water flows again.

Links to the SEADS livelihood objectives

Rehabilitating crop-related infrastructure relates to all three of the SEADS livelihood objectives:

1. to provide immediate livelihood benefits to crop-producing households affected by crisis.
2. to protect crop-related livelihoods of households affected by crisis.
3. to rebuild or support crop-related production, infrastructure, and systems to ensure livelihoods for households affected by crisis.

The extent to which rehabilitating crop-related infrastructure contributes to each objective depends on when it occurs in the crop production cycle. Infrastructure rehabilitation always contributes to Objective 3, as this objective is the least time sensitive.

Whether rehabilitation has an immediate impact on crop production depends on the time of the year. Some infrastructure rehabilitation, when implemented in the aftermath of a crisis, can have an immediate impact on crop-related livelihoods. Activities such as cleaning an irrigation canal, repairing terraces, demining, and clearing debris can therefore contribute directly to Objective 1.

Objective 2 relates to livelihood protection, which can best be done during the preparedness phase by reinforcing infrastructure to make it less vulnerable to hazards (for example, retrofitting buildings or repairing lightly damaged infrastructure to prevent further deterioration), locating it in places of lower vulnerability, or increasing the capacity of water reservoirs to protect crops against droughts. In a conflict context, rehabilitating infrastructure in an inclusive way and supporting crop-related livelihoods that promote trade and communication among different parties will also contribute to Objective 2.

The minimum standards in this chapter focus on:

- avoiding further asset deterioration or losses and ensuring continued production
- ensuring and increasing future production and ability to withstand future shocks
- improving preparedness and recovery by linking to long-term development.

The importance of crop-related infrastructure in crisis response

Crop-related infrastructure is essential at all stages of the crop production cycle. For example:

- Irrigation, terracing, and fencing are essential for crop production.
- Transport and market infrastructure promote linkages between producers and value-chain actors at different stages of the crop production cycle.
- Storage infrastructure and shade structures maintain the quality of inputs and products, and protect equipment and machinery.

Rehabilitating crop-related infrastructure after a crisis may also bring temporary and permanent employment opportunities, increasing the potential of infrastructure rehabilitation to contribute to the recovery of affected communities. Rehabilitation presents an opportunity to make infrastructure less vulnerable to natural or human-induced hazards by considering existing vulnerabilities based on past experiences and predicting and preparing for future hazards.

Rehabilitating crop-related infrastructure requires materials, labor, and technical knowledge and skills. If the required rehabilitation exceeds the affected community's capacity in one or more of these three areas, local government, humanitarian actors, or specialized sub-contractors may need to be involved.

Table 7.1 lists examples of infrastructure used at each stage of crop production, issues that may result from a crisis, and possible solutions.

Table 7.1: Different infrastructure rehabilitation solutions can address issues throughout the crop production cycle

Crop production stage	Issue	Infrastructure solution
Pre-production	Existing crop-related infrastructure is vulnerable to crisis	Protect and retrofit to reduce vulnerability
	Gullies are created or deepened, and terraces are broken, leading to erosion and loss of soil	Repair terraces and fill gullies
	Debris, mines, and unexploded ordnance make it difficult or impossible to prepare land and irrigation	Clear fields and irrigation canals of debris, mines, and unexploded ordnance
	Access to land and infrastructure is impossible due to damage, destruction, or the presence of mines and unexploded ordnance	Rehabilitate or demine roads, bridges, culverts, and other crop-related infrastructure to ensure safe access

...continued

	Access to input sellers is impossible or restricted	Repair and rebuild marketplaces and access roads
Production	Livestock invade fields, compacting soil and eating crops	Repair or provide permanent fences
	Machinery, equipment, and inputs need to be stored safely	Repair or rebuild shades, warehouses, and silos
	Excess water on soil does not allow roots to breathe	Rehabilitate drainage infrastructure
	Lack of water for crops to grow	Rehabilitate irrigation infrastructure (Muthigani et al. 2010)
	Lack of heat and humidity for crops to grow faster or off season	Rehabilitate greenhouses
Post-production	Harvest cannot be transported, as roads are not passable	Rehabilitate or rebuild roads, bridges, and culverts
	Harvest needs to be stored for consumption by the community or until it is sold	Repair, rebuild, or reinforce warehouses and silos
	Marketplaces are destroyed by the crisis so the community has no proper place to sell the harvest	Repair, rebuild, or reinforce market stalls (Marocchino 2009) Rehabilitate interior market roads and drainage

Case Study 7.1 (see SEADS website) provides an example of how rehabilitating a water-harvesting structure can improve crop-related livelihoods.

Technical options for supporting crop-related infrastructure

This chapter presents two technical options and several sub-options for rehabilitating crop-related infrastructure:

- Facilitate community-led infrastructure rehabilitation.
- Lead and implement direct infrastructure rehabilitation.

These two technical options were selected based on available evidence of impact from agriculture responses in humanitarian crisis (SEADS 2021) and on expert opinion. However, evidence did not disaggregate what caused the impact on livelihoods when a combination of response areas and technical options was used. Productivity increases may also result from a combination of response areas.

Evidence indicates that combinations of response areas and technical options can improve livelihood outcomes, either through increased food security, reduced food expenditures, or increased income. See, for example, Mollet 2011, Walter et al. 2017, ICRC 2019, and Trust Consultancy & Development 2020 in the *SEADS Evidence Database*.

Technical Option 1: Facilitate community-led infrastructure rehabilitation

Three sub-options are available:

1.1. Provide the required tools, materials, or funds for the rehabilitation, either as household kits (for crop-related infrastructure at household level) or for the whole community (for community infrastructure, to be managed by local leadership). This sub-option contributes to localization, in line with the Grand Bargain. Coordination with support to crop production through tools, equipment, and other non-seed inputs (Chapter 6: Tools, Equipment, and Other Non-seed Inputs) is essential to ensure relevance of this sub-option and achievement of livelihood impacts.

1.2. Provide legal and technical assistance to secure sustainable access to and use of the infrastructure by all users and to ensure the infrastructure meets the required technical standards. This support can be provided at the household or community level.

1.3. Facilitate employment schemes to complete the rehabilitation. This option is usually most suitable for rehabilitation projects requiring unskilled manual labor in a context of relative stability after a crisis, when the community has a long-term perspective for the rehabilitation work.

Case Study 7.2 (see SEADS website) shows how rehabilitating irrigation schemes can be implemented through a cash-for-work approach.

Technical Option 2: Lead and implement direct infrastructure rehabilitation

This option is likely to be effective in complex or costly rehabilitation projects or because the local policies and laws require it. Two sub-options are available:

2.1.   Organizations do the rehabilitation work themselves, as they have the technical capacity to procure materials and hire and manage skilled laborers.

Case Study 7.3 (see SEADS website) presents an example of direct assistance by the International Committee of the Red Cross (ICRC) to rehabilitate greenhouses in the Gaza Strip.

2.2.   Organizations hire private contractors to do the rehabilitation work.

Option 2 and its sub-options can be used for permanent infrastructure if required, but it is particularly well suited to households in need of livelihood support in an unstable context (for example, internally displaced people, refugees, conflict). In such situations, a rapid rehabilitation can be done if directed by the organization. Option 2 is also likely to be the most feasible for demining, which requires specific equipment and skills and technical knowledge of military tactics and weapons.

Advantages and disadvantages of each technical option

Both technical options ensure that humanitarian principles and livelihood objectives are respected. They incorporate the need to build back better while considering climate change adaptation, local traditional techniques, and local materials and laws. Both options also require operations and maintenance systems to ensure the long-term sustainability of the rehabilitated infrastructure. The advantages and disadvantages of each option are summarized in Table 7.2.

Table 7.2: Each crop-related infrastructure option has advantages and disadvantages

	Advantages	Disadvantages
1. Facilitate community-led rehabilitation	<ul><li>Increased community ownership</li><li>Builds on traditional community-based systems</li><li>Reduced cost due to community contributions (labor, materials)</li><li>Opportunities for capacity building, not only at technical level, but also in local people's management and leadership</li><li>Might be more sustainable if maintenance remains with communities</li></ul>	<ul><li>May be more difficult to manage if there is conflict or tension among different groups in the community or restrictions that limit participation of people according to their ethnicity, gender, religion, or disability</li><li>May keep people away from their own livelihoods or from temporary migration to earn higher income in urban areas or neighboring countries</li><li>May not be possible because the people in the community are busy with their livelihoods or have temporarily migrated</li><li>May present unacceptable safety risks to community members unless they have technical knowledge of mines and unexploded ordnance</li></ul>

...continued

| 2. Lead and implement direct rehabilitation | • Easier to implement a more inclusive scheme
• Can ensure humanitarian standards in respect of labor law, safety norms, child labor, and equal and fair wages
• Builds local capacities if local people are hired
• Can establish a comprehensive operations and maintenance system to ensure sustainability
• Easier to arrange, supervise, and manage
• Can plan and guarantee the quality of the rehabilitation
• Easier to arrange a high level of skills and equipment if required
• Opportunity to bring new, improved technologies to the community | • May undermine traditional community-based systems and create dependency on support
• May compete with local organizations or companies that could also do the rehabilitation
• If done through a sub-contractor from outside the community, the resources paid go out of the community
• If a private contractor is used, the possibility of local capacity building is small
• It is difficult to create a comprehensive operations and maintenance system, as the organization's involvement is limited to short-term contract compliance and supervision |

Timing of crop-related infrastructure technical options

Rehabilitating crop-related infrastructure usually starts in early recovery after a crisis, once essential lifesaving responses are in place or routinely managed. However, if the rehabilitation provides labor opportunities for unskilled workers in the affected community, then in-kind payments or cash and voucher assistance can enable people to meet their basic needs, and the rehabilitation work could be done early in the response.

For a rapid-onset crisis, retrofitting and protection of crop-related infrastructure prior to an expected crisis might be appropriate. Emergency preparedness and early actions can be implemented where a crisis can be predicted or anticipated, such as typhoons and earthquakes.

In a slow-onset crisis, such as a drought, it is sensible to increase the capacity of water deposits and reservoirs for irrigation.

In a complex crisis, there is a risk that rehabilitated infrastructure may be repeatedly damaged. This is particularly the case with conflicts and civil unrest where people's livelihoods are targeted. Therefore, conditions need to be stable enough to reduce the risk of recurrent damage.

The legal and technical assistance sub-option (Technical Option 1.2) might be needed before the rehabilitation work starts to ensure that all stakeholders understand the requirements, with particular attention to the most vulnerable groups. Unlike other technical options, this assistance may continue into recovery if future hazards are anticipated. If they are, assistance should be coordinated with development projects.

Table 7.3 summarizes the most effective timing for rehabilitating crop-related infrastructure in different phases of a crisis.

The crop production cycle has less influence on infrastructure rehabilitation timing than the phase of the crisis or forecasts of future hazards. Nevertheless, infrastructure rehabilitation may require significant community labor, and thus it should avoid times of peak local labor demand, such as the harvest, or of seasonal migration to urban areas or abroad for work. Use seasonal agriculture and labor calendars to identify peak periods. Efficiencies can be gained in implementation by timing infrastructure rehabilitation support with other types of crop-related response. For safety reasons, the removal of mines and unexploded ordnance may need to be done well before the agricultural season.

Table 7.3: Different crop-related infrastructure options are relevant at different phases of a crisis response

TECHNICAL SUB-OPTIONS	Rapid-onset crisis				Slow-onset crisis			
	Preparedness	Immediate aftermath	Early recovery	Recovery	Alert	Alarm	Emergency	Recovery
Option 1.1 Provide tools and materials	———————————————→				——————————→			
Option 1.2 Provide legal and technical assistance	———→		———————→		———→			———→
Option 1.3 Facilitate short-term employment schemes	·····························▶				·······▶			········▶
Option 2.1 Organizations provide services directly	·····························▶				·······▶			········▶
Option 2.2 Organizations hire private contractors	———————————————▶				———→			———→

———→ relevant

·········▶ relevant except during excess rain and high labor demand

Rehabilitation work is usually better done during dry periods as the rain disturbs the work and it takes longer for construction work to dry during the rainy season.

Table 7.4 presents example timelines for infrastructure rehabilitation against the stages of crop production.

Decision tree to select technical options

A decision tree can guide your choice of technical options. It prompts you to consider the variables in a systematic way. Decision tree questions are ordered in terms of priority to program quality.

Answer Question 1 first (either "yes" or "no"). The decision tree directs you to a new question based on your answer. "No" responses indicate that other suitable responses identified in the Response-area identification tool (RAIT) should be considered or that further training or capacity building may be required to answer "yes" to the questions.

Table 7.4: Different crop-related infrastructure options are relevant at different stages of the agriculture calendar

TECHNICAL SUB-OPTIONS	STAGE OF THE CROP PRODUCTION CYCLE DURING WHICH THE RESPONSE WILL OCCUR			
	Pre-production planning (for example, crop or seed selection)	**Production** (for example, land preparation, crop management)	**Post-production** (for example, harvesting, storage, processing)	**Marketing** (for example, market access, transport)
Option 1.1 Provide tools and materials	———————→		———————→	
Option 1.2 Provide legal and technical assistance	——————————————————————→			
Option 1.3 Facilitate short-term employment schemes	···▶			
Option 2.1 Organizations provide services directly	·······························▶ ——————————→			
Option 2.2 Organizations hire private contractors	·······························▶ ——————————→			

———→ relevant

·········▶ relevant except during excess rain and high labor demand

Your answers should be based on all data at your disposal, but in particular:

- the results of the initial assessment (see Chapter 4: Initial Assessment for Crop-related Crisis Response)
- a theory of change (see Minimum Standard 8.2: Project objectives)
- your organization's capacity to achieve relevant minimum standards in this chapter (see Annex B).

SEADS recommends that you complete a RAIT (see Minimum Standard 4.4: Selecting response areas) before completing a decision tree. The RAIT will indicate whether crop-related infrastructure responses are necessary, appropriate, and feasible, and which livelihood objective they may have the greatest impact on.

Use Figure 7.1 to test whether crop-related infrastructure should be part of a crop-related response and, if so, which technical options will be most appropriate.

Figure 7.1: Decision tree for crop-related infrastructure

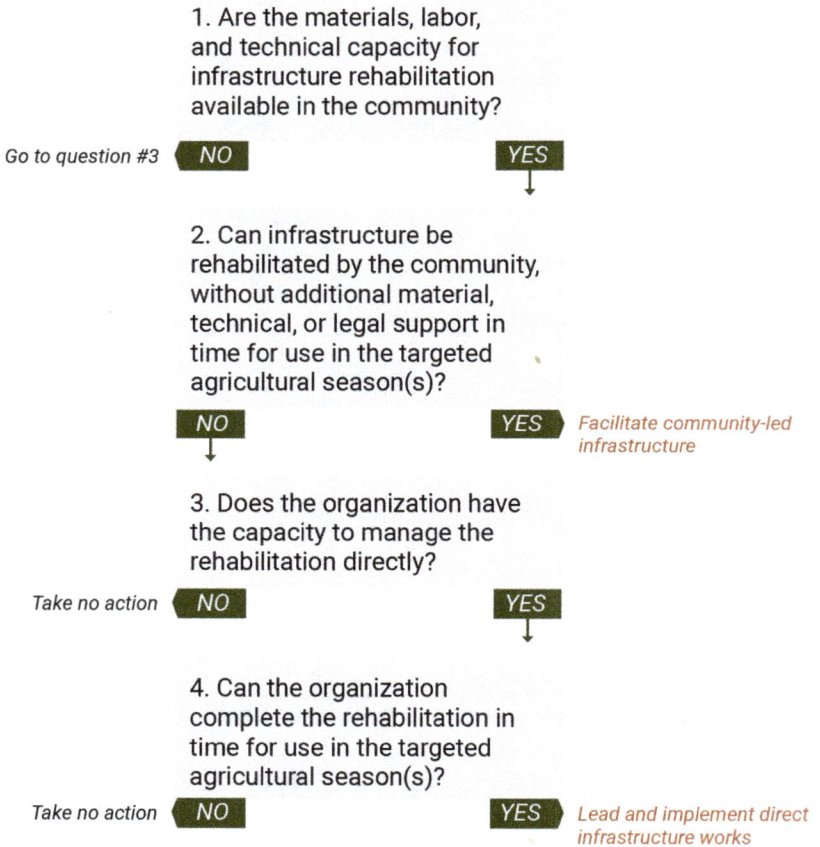

1. Are the materials, labor, and technical capacity for infrastructure rehabilitation available in the community?

Go to question #3 NO   YES

2. Can infrastructure be rehabilitated by the community, without additional material, technical, or legal support in time for use in the targeted agricultural season(s)?

NO   YES *Facilitate community-led infrastructure*

3. Does the organization have the capacity to manage the rehabilitation directly?

Take no action NO   YES

4. Can the organization complete the rehabilitation in time for use in the targeted agricultural season(s)?

Take no action NO   YES *Lead and implement direct infrastructure works*

Note: The result *Take no action* does not necessarily mean that no response should take place, but rather that other suitable responses identified in the RAIT should be considered or further training or capacity building may be required to answer "yes" to the questions. Where no other suitable options exist and training and capacity building is not possible, support to alternative livelihoods can be considered.

Crop-related infrastructure minimum standards

Minimum Standard 7.1: Assessment and planning

Assessment identifies the key infrastructure rehabilitation needs and the technical requirements for implementing.

Key actions

- Identify the key infrastructure constraints as well as factors to consider in determining the most appropriate and timely response (see Guidance notes 1, 2, and 3).

- Consider the positive and negative environmental impacts of the infrastructure rehabilitation (see Guidance note 3).

- Understand the local legislation, preferred construction techniques, materials, and building codes. Use them for the design and planning of the rehabilitation work (see Guidance notes 3 and 4).

- Understand existing ownership and access inequalities and consider ways to overcome them (see Guidance note 5).

- Collect the relevant information to build back better so that the rehabilitation work reduces vulnerability to future crises (see Guidance notes 6 and 7).

- Ensure staff have relevant technical competencies and provide training to fill gaps (see Annex B).

- Use Appendix 4.1: Example questions to gather initial and technical data and Appendix 7.1: Initial assessment checklist for crop-related infrastructure responses to select assessment questions.

Guidance notes

1. **Initial assessment.** Assess the context for crop-related infrastructure rehabilitation, including the level of damage to critical crop-related infrastructure as a result of the crisis and the community's capacity to support rehabilitation work. Consult broadly to understand ownership, access, and use of the infrastructure.

Clarify who will benefit from the rehabilitation work and how the crisis response will help those most vulnerable meet their basic needs and/or recover their livelihoods (see SEADS Principle 2: Use a participatory approach in all aspects of crisis response and Chapter 4).

2.   **Market assessment**. As a component of initial assessment, a market assessment is an opportunity to collect relevant information on materials and services available locally for the rehabilitation work. This includes information about seasonal labor availability and demand, wages, construction materials, and local contractors in the market. For planning the rehabilitation, it's useful to have information on labor and resource availability, cost, and quality, as well as on the reliability of supply. That information allows you to avoid creating scarcity at the local level.

3.   **Environmental assessment**. Initial assessment should include information about relevant environmental aspects regarding the location of the infrastructure, sourcing of tools, equipment, and materials, and management and disposal of any by-products and debris. Understand and comply with local environmental legislation and avoid negative impacts on the environment (see SEADS Principle 4: Consider climate change and minimize environmental impacts).

4.   **Local legislation, norms, and building codes**. The assessment should provide an understanding of local practices, traditions, techniques, technology, norms, and specifications for infrastructure construction and rehabilitation. This will identify potential constraints posed by some response options and can identify the need for legal advice to clarify technical requirements and issues relating to ownership of, access to, and use of crop-related infrastructure. Such information will also be useful when organizing operations and maintenance post-rehabilitation.

5.   **Equity**. Historical inequalities in the community will probably be reflected in the location of, ownership of, and access to crop-related infrastructure. For example, it is probably located closer to wealthier, more influential members of the community. By comparison, more vulnerable users will typically live farther away from the infrastructure, increasing their travel costs, time, and exposure to protection risks. Ownership and access may also be limited by gender and ethnicity. It is difficult to change and challenge sociocultural norms in a crisis response, particularly one characterized by existing conflict. However, understanding the power system that created those sociocultural norms may help to increase inclusiveness and promote some actions to address them (see SEADS Principle 1: Use livelihoods-based programming).

6.   **Build back better**. Infrastructure rehabilitation is an opportunity to provide the community with better and more resilient infrastructure that can withstand future

crises. Building codes define how strong and resilient the infrastructure should be. The assessment should identify the relevant codes from the local legislation and use them for planning and design. Building back better can also include consideration of opportunities to improve technologies, especially consideration of green technologies, such as replacing a diesel-engine pump with a solar-powered pump. While many donors tend to prioritize rehabilitation, especially in protracted crises where the infrastructure no longer exists, new construction can enable faster recovery and provide a foundation for development.

7.   **Disaster risk mapping.** Within a community, some locations are more vulnerable to certain hazards than others (for example, flood plains or a location near a gasoline deposit). The assessment should map all these risks and vulnerability to hazards so that they are considered in the response design and planning (CRS 2017).

Sometimes, governments may revise policies after a crisis to reduce impacts should a similar crisis occur again. For example, after the Indian Ocean earthquake and tsunami in 2004, the Sri Lankan government created a buffer zone to prevent organizations from rehabilitating close to the sea. New and revised regulations have an important impact on any rehabilitation plan.

Climate change will lead to increasingly frequent and powerful crises. Therefore, assessments made on the basis of previous events may be misleading because the next event may be more extreme. Use Climate change projections done by a reputable institution or the government to design and plan an appropriate response. Be aware that building codes may be revised in response to those same predictions.

Minimum Standard 7.2: Technical specifications

The rehabilitated infrastructure is safe, meets the required local technical specifications, and is appropriate for the intended use.

Key actions

- Confirm that the identified technical option complies with the applicable planning and building codes, material specifications, and quality specifications (see Guidance notes 1 and 2).

- Increase the technical capacity of local people, which will increase the sustainability of the rehabilitation and reduce the need for external assistance in the future (see Guidance note 3).

- Build back better and promote safe rehabilitation practices to meet needs and reduce future risks (see Guidance note 4).

- Establish an appropriate project management system and establish an operations and maintenance system for sustainability of the infrastructure (see Guidance note 5).

- Assess environmental baseline conditions and identify available local resources and environmental hazards. Minimize negative environmental impacts during infrastructure rehabilitation, operation, and eventual decommissioning. Incorporate an environmental management plan into operations and maintenance procedures (see Guidance note 6).

- Coordinate with other organizations to optimize infrastructure rehabilitation practices and local livelihood opportunities (see Guidance note 7).

Guidance notes

1.   Local building codes. Local building codes should reflect local culture, climatic conditions, resources, local materials, and maintenance capacities, as well as accessibility and affordability. For household-level infrastructure, ensure that infrastructure rehabilitation allows users to meet the required codes and specifications. Where there are no existing specifications, use United Nations standards. Establish minimum specifications in collaboration with the local authorities and relevant stakeholders to ensure they meet safety and performance requirements. Where relevant and possible, relocate crop-related infrastructure to avoid future damage or destruction from future crises. If the location cannot be changed, consider opportunities to apply specifications beyond those in any existing building codes.

2.   Sourcing materials. Sourcing materials locally may affect the local economy, environment, or availability of labor. Sometimes adequate materials may not be available locally and other alternatives may need to be used. If this happens, consider the impact of using materials that are unfamiliar to the local culture. Ensure that environmental concerns are addressed and promote reuse of salvaged materials. Select the most sustainable materials among the viable options. Prefer those that do not deplete local natural resources or contribute to long-term environmental damage (see SEADS Principle 4).

3. **Local competencies and participation.** Infrastructure rehabilitation should be compatible with local practices. That requires ongoing engagement with people affected by the crisis (see SEADS Principle 2). Training programs and apprenticeship schemes can maximize opportunities for affected people to participate directly in infrastructure rehabilitation. Provide opportunities for women and persons with disabilities to participate. People less able to undertake physical tasks can contribute to complementary activities such as site monitoring. Training and awareness-raising builds technical capacity among the affected populations, local authorities, local building professionals, skilled and unskilled labor, landlords, and local partners. In locations vulnerable to seasonal or cyclical hazards, involve local experts who have knowledge of and experience with local rehabilitation practices, building codes, and suitable materials.

Case Study 7.4 (see SEADS website) illustrates how active involvement and participation increases competencies at the community level.

4. **Build back better.** Initial assessment should identify why the infrastructure failed or was damaged or destroyed. It should also identify ways to avoid this failure, damage, or destruction happening again. This requires an understanding of the vulnerability of the infrastructure location to similar future events. Consider the impact of climate change based on existing studies and projections. climate change may have an additional negative impact on vulnerability to hazards, which will require additional protection. The assessment may suggest that moving the infrastructure to another location is an option for reducing future vulnerability.

5. **Project management.** Develop a rehabilitation plan or calendar that includes target milestones and start and completion dates. The schedule should note the onset of seasonal weather and include a contingency plan for unforeseen events. Set up a management and monitoring system for materials, labor, and site supervision. This should address sourcing, procurement, transportation, handling, and administration throughout the process. Develop a comprehensive operations and maintenance plan to ensure effective long-term operation. Key components of a plan include users' participation, defining roles and responsibilities, and having a cost-recovery or cost-sharing plan. For repairs, check that materials and spare parts are available in the market, as well as local technicians with the skills to make the required repairs.

6. **Environmental protection.** Environmental protection associated with infrastructure rehabilitation should reflect SEADS Principle 4. For example, stabilize the soil by retaining vegetation, using natural contours for roads, pathways, and drainage networks, and establishing drainage systems under roadways or planted

earth banks. Debris management activities immediately after the crisis should promote safe disposal or reuse, depending on local attitudes and the proximity of businesses willing to purchase the debris. Minimize the use of non-renewable energy and promote the use of renewable energy sources. Include energy-efficient designs using passive approaches for heating and cooling.

7. **Linkages to other humanitarian standards.** Rehabilitating crop-related infrastructure might overlap with other humanitarian actions. Consider the potential implications and synergies as well as relevant humanitarian standards (see SEADS Principle 5: Establish coordinated responses). For example, rehabilitating irrigation infrastructure and water deposits for livelihoods use may increase access to potable water. However, it may also create breeding places for disease vectors, such as mosquitos. Infrastructure rehabilitation is also likely to benefit from close cooperation with organizations engaged in shelter and settlements projects.

Minimum Standard 7.3: Location, lifetime, and timing

Crop-related rehabilitated infrastructure is located in the right place at the right time and meets the required lifetime for its users.

Key actions

- Decide if the infrastructure should be temporary or permanent (see Guidance note 1).
- Locate the infrastructure in the most suitable place from a functional, accessibility, protection, and equity perspective (see Guidance notes 2 and 3).
- Time the infrastructure rehabilitation so it is available, accessible, and ready to use at the right time (see Guidance notes 4 and 5).

Guidance notes

1. **Lifetime requirements of the infrastructure.** Crop-related infrastructure may be required for a defined period of time or for as long as possible. For instance, refugees or internally displaced people may be in a camp for several months or years, giving them the opportunity to grow and market crops; for that they need crop-related infrastructure on a temporary basis. Temporary infrastructure may also be appropriate for a community affected by a complex crisis, as the additional investment required for permanent infrastructure may be difficult to justify given that it could be again damaged or destroyed during the crisis. The decision on which option to choose should be based on the initial assessment, the technical options available, and benefit-cost analysis. The rehabilitation of permanent infrastructure typically requires the use of specialized technology, a longer implementation timeframe, strong community participation, and linkages to the sustainable development of the community. At the same time, it should contribute to or fit into the national development plan. Permanent infrastructure should have an agreed lifespan and a decommissioning plan, ideally developed at the design phase of the response. On the other hand, temporary infrastructure will require higher technical skills and materials that will need to be implemented directly by the organization or a specialized sub-contractor (Technical Option 2). Temporary infrastructure may need to be easily mountable and dismountable, requiring specialized skills, materials, and financial resources. For example, a temporary warehouse may use a metallic structure while a permanent one would use concrete, which is much cheaper and the materials, funds, and skills are more likely to be locally available. Some temporary infrastructure, such as fences, could be treated like a tool or equipment by the organization. See Chapter 6 for guidance.

2. **Location of the infrastructure.** The location of the infrastructure should allow people to use it appropriately, safely, and in a timely manner. For household-level infrastructure, each household can decide where to locate it within their property. For community-level infrastructure, location needs to be discussed and agreed in consultation with representatives of all the people and institutions involved. When determining the best location for community-level infrastructure, consider property rights, ownership, and potential benefits for vulnerable groups (see SEADS Principle 1).Consider any protection risks for the users of collective crop-related infrastructure. Users should not be put at risk when traveling from home to the infrastructure. If possible, minimize the distance to travel and provide night lighting. Provide appropriate fire safety equipment and training, as well as evacuation plans and escape routes. Locations near industrial hazards, including fuel storage facilities, pose unnecessary risks and are best avoided. If they cannot be avoided, appropriate risk reduction measures will be required. Similarly, in

conflict areas, locating the infrastructure near a military base or the house of an authority may also affect the security and safety of those using the infrastructure.

3. **Protection and equity considerations.** Consider all-weather access, security risks, and potential access restrictions due to gender, ethnicity, religious affiliation, disability, or other sociocultural barriers, such as language or literacy (see the Protection Principles in the *Sphere Handbook*).

4. **Timing of the rehabilitation.** Ideally, rehabilitation of crop-related infrastructure should align with the local agriculture calendar. For instance, rehabilitate the irrigation canals before the crops need to be watered and ensure silos are available before the grains are harvested. In general, it is easier to do rehabilitation work during dry periods, as the rain may disrupt the work and delay completion. Conflict situations may also impose unavoidable constraints on timing, including the risk that the infrastructure may be destroyed during the conflict. Transport infrastructure, such as roads and bridges, is frequently targeted by warring parties. However, be aware that any delays in infrastructure rehabilitation affect the speed with which local crop-based livelihoods can return to normal. For security reasons, mines and unexploded ordnance may need to be removed as soon as possible, regardless of the agricultural season.

5. **Conflict reduction and peace building.** Rehabilitating crop-related infrastructure at the right time protects existing livelihoods, speeds up their recovery, and promotes trade among different and diverse communities. That increases communication and cooperation between those communities, reducing the possibility of future conflicts.

Recommended reading

Details of references cited in this chapter are in Annex C. Further recommended reading includes:

Catholic Relief Services (2013). *Toward resilience: A guide to disaster risk reduction and climate change adaptation.* Practical Action Publishing. https://www.crs.org/our-work-overseas/research-publications/toward-resilience

International Committee of the Red Cross (ICRC) (2016). *EcoSec review report: ILOT Gaza – Greenhouse rehabilitation project.* https://seads-standards.org/wp-content/uploads/2021/04/Asia_04-ICRC-ILOT-Greenhouse-rehabilitation.pdf

ICRC (2019). *EcoSec post distribution monitoring report: ILOT – Rehabilitation of rainwater harvesting ponds in Abssan and Khuzaa border areas of Gaza Strip.* https://seads-standards.org/wp-content/uploads/2021/04/Asia_06-ICRC-ILOT-Rehabilitation-rainwater.pdf

ICRC (2019). *EcoSec project review report: ILOT – Rehabilitation of agricultural lands in the border area (100–300 m) from the security fence.* Summary report. https://seads-standards.org/wp-content/uploads/2021/05/Asia_03-ICRC-Approved-Summary-Review-report-ILOT-Land-rehabilitation.pdf

Mendelsohn, R. (2009). The impact of climate change on agriculture in developing countries. *Journal of natural resources policy research 1*, 5–19. https://doi.org/10.1080/19390450802495882

Robillard, S., Atim, T. & Maxwell, D. (2021). *Localization: A "Landscape" report.* Feinstein International Center, Friedman School of Nutrition Science and Policy at Tufts University. https://fic.tufts.edu/publication-item/localization-a-landscape-report/

SEEP Network (2017). *Minimum economic recovery standards* (3rd edn.). Practical Action Publishing. https://doi.org/10.3362/9781780446707

Stern, P. (1979). *Small-scale irrigation.* Intermediate Technology Publications. https://doi.org/10.3362/9781780443362

Swiss Agency for Development and Cooperation (2008). *Manual for manufacturing metal silos for grain storage.* https://postharvest.nri.org/images/documents/Metal_silos/Metal_silo_manual_English.pdf

Tembo, S. & Blokhuis, F. (no date). *Manual for supervision of labour based road rehabilitation works.* ILO ASIST. http://www.ilo.org/wcmsp5/groups/public/---ed_emp/---emp_policy/---invest/documents/instructionalmaterial/wcms_asist_8051.pdf

UNOCHA (2011). *Disaster waste management guidelines.* Joint United Nations Environment Program/OCHA Environment Unit. https://www.unocha.org/sites/unocha/files/DWMG.pdf

Appendix 7.1: Initial assessment checklist for crop-related infrastructure responses

These are suggested questions to ask when planning to rehabilitate crop-related infrastructure. The objective is to ensure that the minimum data are collected for assessment and response identification so that the rehabilitation plan and implementation of the crop-related infrastructure meets the SEADS minimum standards. None of the questions is mandatory. Adapt the list to suit the context.

Assessment and planning

1. What secondary data are already available on the affected community about crop-related infrastructure rehabilitation?
2. What are the local specifications, building codes, and local technologies available for infrastructure rehabilitation?
3. Who are the owners of the crop-related infrastructure? Are there any ownership certificates or titles? Have these titles been affected by the crisis?
4. What are the local regulations for the use of, management of, and access to the infrastructure? Any restrictions to some parts of the population?
5. Have the local authorities made any recent post-crisis legal changes to land use or construction specifications due to the crisis that could affect the rehabilitation work?
6. Which crop-related infrastructure has been affected by the crisis? What is the extent of the damage? How technical is the likely fix?
7. What constraints does that damage place on crop producers' ability to carry out normal pre-production, production, post-production, and marketing activities?
8. In the current location, how vulnerable is the crop-related infrastructure to crisis and disasters (natural and human-made), including climate change? How can this vulnerability be reduced?
9. What material, financial, and human resources are available to meet some or all of the infrastructure rehabilitation needs?

10. What is the seasonal labor calendar in the community? When is unskilled labor available and unavailable? What is the daily wage and its variation throughout the year? What is the labor law for short-term employment schemes?
11. Is there skilled labor in the community? Is it available and sufficient? How does availability change throughout the year? What is the wage for skilled labor?
12. Are there local companies or consultants with the skills to undertake infrastructure rehabilitation?
13. Would people in the community participate in vocational training and short-term employment schemes?

Materials, design, and construction

1. What initial solutions or materials have the affected users or other actors provided?
2. What existing materials can be salvaged from the damaged site for use in the rehabilitation?
3. What are the typical rehabilitation practices of the affected people, and what materials do they use?
4. In normal times, when is rehabilitation, repair, and construction work traditionally done in the year?
5. How can women, youth, persons with disabilities, and older people be trained or assisted to participate in the rehabilitation work? What are the constraints?
6. Are there any legal requirements or restrictions for harvesting or purchasing rehabilitation materials? Could the rehabilitation harm the local environment if these legal requirements are not considered? For example, purchase of bamboo or timber from protected forest.
7. Are tools, spare parts, and construction materials of the required quality and at affordable prices available in the local market? Is availability and cost constant throughout the year or does it vary? If it varies, how?

CHAPTER 8:
IMPACT-ORIENTED MONITORING AND EVALUATION

Minimum standards: impact-oriented monitoring and evaluation

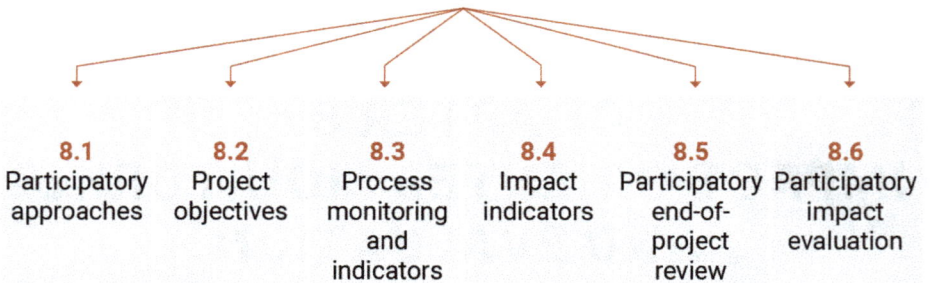

8.1 Participatory approaches	8.2 Project objectives	8.3 Process monitoring and indicators	8.4 Impact indicators	8.5 Participatory end-of-project review	8.6 Participatory impact evaluation

> Annex A: Glossary contains definitions of some of the technical terms used in SEADS.

This chapter describes the minimum standards for the monitoring and evaluation of crop-related crisis responses. There is a need for more impact evaluation of crop-related crisis responses, while also recognizing the operational challenges and the diversity of actors in humanitarian contexts. At present, many organizations focus on monitoring project implementation and expenditure, rather than impact.

Impact evaluation in crop-related crisis responses is challenging because:

- Livelihood impacts are often not expected until many months after a crop-related crisis response ends, particularly for short-term projects that respond to a rapid-onset crisis.
- Supporting crop production does not automatically lead to livelihood impacts.

The SEADS minimum standards recognize that most humanitarian organizations already have monitoring and evaluation systems in place. However, these systems are seldom specific to crop-related responses. The minimum standards in this chapter provide guidance on how to refine existing systems to improve understanding of crop-related responses.

Impact-oriented monitoring and evaluation minimum standards

Minimum Standard 8.1: Participatory approaches

Active community participation is part of monitoring and impact evaluation of crop-related crisis responses.

Key actions

- Work jointly with communities to agree to expected impacts of crop-related responses and identify relevant impact indicators (see Guidance note 1).
- Involve communities actively in the monitoring of response implementation and in end-of-project reviews and impact evaluations of crop-related crisis responses (see Guidance note 2).
- Use locally appropriate participatory methods during monitoring and impact evaluation (see Guidance note 3).
- Ensure that vulnerable and disadvantaged groups are involved in monitoring and impact evaluation (see Guidance note 4).

Guidance notes

1.   Impacts and impact indicators. Participatory initial assessment should lead to a rapid understanding of the role of crop production in livelihoods, the crop production cycle, and specific crop production practices. As responses are identified and discussed, the likely impacts of these responses can also be discussed. An initial assessment is therefore an opportunity to gather information for the design of monitoring and evaluation activities and the selection of impact indicators. Example questions in Appendix 4.1 will support data collection to monitor impacts. Appendix 8.1 provides examples of impact indicators.

2.   Participatory monitoring, review, and impact evaluation. In line with SEADS Principle 2: Use a participatory approach in all aspects of crisis response. Participatory approaches should be used for monitoring, impact evaluation, end-of-project reviews, and learning activities. participatory approaches, such as focus group discussions, key informant interviews, and proportional piling, require working relationships with communities that involve joint identification of relevant impacts (see Guidance note 1). They also require regular meetings and dialogue during response implementation to jointly track planned and actual implementation and discuss any changes to the response. An end-of-project review (see Minimum Standard 8.5) or impact evaluation (see Minimum Standard 8.6) should also use participatory approaches to compare actual results to the project objectives. Appendix 8.2 illustrates various participatory methods that can be used to monitor, review, or evaluate crop-related crisis responses.

3.   Qualitative and quantitative data. Participatory methods are commonly associated with qualitative information. However, they can also produce quantitative information, such as market prices, crop production data, or proportion of income derived from crop sales. Some of this information can be cross-checked with secondary data, such as earlier livelihood or food security assessments and research reports or statistics from local agriculture offices or markets. Larger development projects often use quantitative baseline surveys in monitoring and evaluation. However, quantitative surveys contradict SEADS Principle 2 of participation. Even in development projects, quantitative surveys are relatively uncommon and tend to be used by larger organizations with relatively more financial and human resources. In crises, the added value of quantitative baselines over rapid participatory assessment is open to question, especially if quantitative information can be obtained from participatory methods and secondary data.

4. **Vulnerable and disadvantaged groups.** An important aspect of community participation is understanding the needs of marginalized or vulnerable groups within communities and tailoring responses accordingly. Inclusive monitoring can mean holding separate meetings with poorer households or people who are marginalized due to ethnicity, faith, gender, disability, or other reasons. Design and implement project reviews and impact evaluations in ways that enable marginalized and vulnerable groups to participate, such as by using participatory methods specifically with these groups. Information collected during monitoring, reviews, and impact evaluations should be disaggregated according to local contexts and the presence of marginalized sub-groups within communities.

Minimum Standard 8.2: Project objectives

The design of crop-related crisis responses shows clear technical plausibility of livelihood impacts as the basis for monitoring and impact evaluation.

Key actions

- Use specific, measurable, achievable, relevant, and time-bound (SMART) project objectives to express and quantify expected livelihood impacts (see Guidance note 1).
- Incorporate SMART objectives into project design tools, such as a theory of change or logical framework (see Guidance note 2).

Guidance notes

1.   **SMART objectives.** A monitoring and evaluation system that supports learning about livelihood impacts should include objectives that state and quantify the intended livelihood impacts on specific households within a specific timeframe. SMART objectives are an important outcome of good-quality initial assessment and response identification. As explained in Chapter 2: The Scope and Approach of SEADS, crop-related crisis response should aim to achieve one or more of the SEADS livelihood objectives. Therefore, SMART objectives at the project level should directly relate to one or more of the SEADS livelihood objectives. They should also align with the SEADS principles in Chapter 3: SEADS Principles. See Tables 5.5, 5.6, 6.5, 6.6, 7.3, and 7.4 for considerations related to timing for different response areas.

Appendix 8.3 provides an example of applying SMART objectives to a crop-related crisis response. In this example, key information for developing the SMART objective is drawn from participatory initial assessment and response identification activities at community level (see Minimum Standard 4.2: Initial assessment approach). This approach is efficient in humanitarian situations because it does not require return visits to the project areas for the purpose of designing a monitoring and evaluation system or collecting baseline data; the key livelihood impacts have already been identified jointly with local stakeholders during the initial assessment and response identification.

2.   **Technical plausibility and theory of change.** SMART objectives indicate whether a project objective is technically plausible, which means that a stated type of response, timing, and amount of inputs (including services, repairs, and reconstruction) will likely lead to an expected impact at household level. During project design, technical plausibility can be demonstrated using simple project design tools, such as a theory of change or logical framework. Different organizations have different preferences for the use of these tools, and there are various versions of each tool. When used properly a theory of change (or logical framework) will show:

- the technical plausibility of project inputs leading to project livelihood impacts
- how project managers can identify and prioritize items that need to be monitored and the frequency of monitoring
- the key predicted livelihood impacts in a quantified form and in terms of when these impacts should occur
- the key assumptions and risks that affect the progression of inputs to impacts; these assumptions and risks need to be tracked during the project.

In crisis responses, attention to technical plausibility and use of a theory of change are especially useful because livelihood impacts are often predicted to occur months after a project ends. In these cases, participatory end-of-project reviews can ensure some understanding of likely impacts, even if an impact evaluation is not possible.

Appendix 8.4 is an example of a simple theory of change for a crop-related crisis response that delivered seeds and fertilizer. This example shows that a theory of change does not need to be complex in order to show technical plausibility and that various assumptions and risks affect how crop production leads to livelihood impacts. The theory of change also indicates areas of additional support that a project might provide to try to reduce the risk of low impact. For example, if there is a high risk of households selling the inputs to meet their basic food needs, the project could consider adding food or cash transfers to prevent seed sale.

A detailed example of technical plausibility is available in Case Study 8.1 (see SEADS website).

Minimum Standard 8.3: Process monitoring and indicators

Regular and systematic process monitoring allows tracking of and adjustments to response implementation, and ensures alignment with SEADS minimum standards.

Key actions

- Monitor process indicators to check the progress of response implementation, check alignment with SEADS minimum standards, and make real-time adjustments as needed (see Guidance note 1).
- Integrate the tracking of context and response risks and assumptions into routine process monitoring (see Guidance note 2).
- Update the response area identification tool (RAIT), the decision trees, and the theory of change as implementation evolves (see Guidance note 3).

Guidance notes

1.   **Process indicators**. This type of indicator measures the progress of response implementation, or what is being done. In most crop-related crisis responses, monitoring focuses on measuring inputs using process indicators. This often involves simple counts of people targeted and/or reached or items provided. Examples include the amounts of inputs provided to target households, the value of vouchers distributed, or the length of irrigation channels rehabilitated. The timing and duration of activities is also commonly included in process indicators. Process indicators track the quality and accountability of implementation. They:

- assist project managers to track response implementation and, when needed, make timely adjustments
- often relate to project expenditure and so support financial accountability of a project
- contribute to impact evaluation by describing activities relative to the project design and implementation plan; this enables predictions of outcomes and impact to be revised if needed.

Process indicators are used to check how implementation aligns with SEADS minimum standards. Examples of key process indicators for relevant minimum standards are provided in Appendix 8.5.

Use process indicators to monitor response implementation regularly, according to organizational and donor requirements. When combined with community focus groups and tracking of risks and assumptions, process monitoring enables timely adjustments to response implementation.

2.   **Context, assumptions, and risks tracking.** During response implementation, the wider context can change, requiring adjustments in project design. Therefore, it is important to track the operational context over time as well as the assumptions and risks in the project theory of change or logframe, and make adjustments to project implementation as needed. Checks on project implementation can involve activities such as community focus groups. This dialogue can include the use of a checklist of assumptions and risks, drawn from the theory of change. It can also potentially expose the exploitation of children, which is covered by the Child Protection Minimum Standard on child labor (The Alliance 2020). As illustrated in Figure A8.1, some assumptions and risks are constant throughout the project, whereas others are only relevant at certain phases of the project. Therefore, the checklist can vary over time to cover topics that are relevant at each phase. In insecure environments, very frequent tracking of the security situation might be

needed such as daily reviews of security issues. Tracking is particularly important when a crisis is complex, long term, or slow onset, and whenever the context changes.

3.   **Updating decision support tools during implementation.** As implementation progresses, the crop, crisis, or operational context may change significantly. Participatory approaches to process monitoring will provide early signals of these changes. Return to your completed RAIT (see Minimum Standard 4.4: Selecting response areas) when changes are evident to ensure that a crop-related response remains necessary, appropriate, and feasible. Review your responses to questions in the decision trees to ensure that your selected technical option remains likely to have livelihood impacts. It is particularly important to update the assumptions and risks that are included in your theory of change as they can also change over time. A survey done by the Global Food Security Cluster's Agriculture Working Group (2022) of partners engaged in crop-responses in 2022 indicated that approximately 40% of partners engage with farmers at some level to monitor outcomes and see if anything needs to change in the project. However, 78% of partners say that more and better engagement is needed.

Minimum Standard 8.4: Impact indicators

Response reviews and impact evaluations use meaningful impact indicators.

Key actions

- Select livelihood impact indicators for crop-related crisis response that directly show impacts on households (see Guidance note 1).

- Select indicators that show impacts on pre-existing systems, services, or markets where relevant (see Guidance note 2).

- Ensure that household-level livelihood impacts are meaningful (see Guidance note 3).

Guidance notes

1.   **Household-level impact indicators.** In general, household-level impact indicators are not well defined or used in crop-related crisis responses. SEADS aims to ensure that responses have livelihood impacts, and these impacts tend to coincide with one or more of the five main assets in typical livelihood frameworks: financial, natural, physical, human, and social. Definitions of these assets, and specific examples of livelihood impact indicators are provided in Appendix 8.1. Further reading at the end of this chapter provides additional examples of process indicators (Appendix 8.5).

Some organizations use a composite index, such as a coping strategy index or a dietary diversity score, to measure impact. In terms of participatory approaches, a challenge with these measures is that populations affected by a crisis are unlikely to propose them as indicators of livelihood impact. Instead, local people tend to express intended crop-related impacts in terms of basic needs, such as amounts of money and food or shares of income and self-sufficiency. Where possible, use impact indicators that are based on local expressions and needs and which all stakeholders will understand (see SEADS Principle 2). A composite index may be useful to measure vulnerability or for comparability across time and space as a basis for learning.

In contrast to process monitoring, it is usually not efficient to measure impact indicators during the implementation of crop-related crisis responses. This is because livelihood impacts are most likely to occur toward the end of a response or after it ends. Impact indicators can be measured during impact evaluation, and the analysis of the findings can be supported by collated process-monitoring data and records of any changes during implementation.

Case Study 8.2 (see SEADS website) provides examples of crop-related responses that led to impacts on household incomes.

2.   **Other impact indicators**. SEADS Principle 1: Use livelihoods-based programming highlights the need for crop-related crisis responses to support pre-existing systems, services, and markets where possible. Therefore, livelihood impact indicators can also measure impacts on systems, services, and markets. See examples in Appendix 8.1.

3.   **Meaningful impact indicators**. Impact indicators for crop-related crisis responses are usually quantitative, expressing impact in terms of an absolute number, such as "average household income from crop sales." However, this

indicator has limited meaning unless it is related to a reference point, which in this case could be "total required household income" or "income required from crop sales." Similarly, a project might report that a household consumed 30 kg of maize that was produced because of project support. But this measure has limited meaning unless the household size and composition is known and the period of consumption is stated. A stronger indicator would relate the maize consumption to the household's nutritional needs.

Further examples of meaningful impact indicators with a reference point are provided in Appendix 8.1.

Minimum Standard 8.5: Participatory end-of-project review

A participatory end-of-project review predicts future livelihood impacts.

Key actions

- Conduct a participatory end-of-project review if livelihood impacts are expected months after a project ends (see Guidance note 1).
- Consider using benefit-cost analysis to complement a participatory end-of-project review (see Guidance note 2).

Guidance notes

1. **Participatory end-of-project review.** A participatory end-of-project review is needed for projects for which the main livelihood impacts are expected months after a project ends. In these situations, the implementing organization might no longer be present, or might not have the resources to evaluate future impacts. The end-of-project review is an opportunity for community members and project staff to review the implementation process, including the theory of change (or logical framework) and risks and assumptions that were applied. participants can also consider if the completed project is likely to achieve the desired livelihood impacts, even though those impacts may not yet be evident. The end-of-project review need not be elaborate or time-consuming; it can simply involve community meetings

supported by collated process-monitoring data and records of risks and assumptions. Simple ranking or scoring tools can assess the likelihood that project impacts will be achieved, assuming that certain conditions remain in place.

This type of predictive review process is imperfect because future events are uncertain. In general, the longer the time between the end of the project and the expected impacts, the greater the likelihood of impact predictions being inaccurate. However, a well-documented end-of-project review can contribute to learning and future project design.

Some organizations have a long-term presence in the areas where crop-related crisis responses are used. Two common situations are long-term development projects and repeated short-term humanitarian projects in a complex crisis. In both situations, this continued presence can enable follow-up of previous crop-related crisis responses many months after the responses took place. This follow-up can involve repeating the end-of-project review process, or a participatory impact evaluation (see Minimum Standard 8.6).

2. **Benefit-cost analysis.** In some situations, benefit-cost analysis can complement a participatory review. In livelihoods-based programming there is often a trade-off between the number of people or households who receive support and the type or amount of support they receive. If a donor or organization prioritizes the number of beneficiaries over the quality or relevance of the support, there is a risk that large numbers of households will receive support that is not sufficient to support livelihoods. Benefit-cost analysis can provide useful information on the cost efficiency of a response for a given level of livelihood impact. It can also identify program costs that can be reduced without substantially reducing the impacts. This can lead to future programs being designed to provide similar livelihood benefits to a larger number of people. When applied to different responses in similar socioeconomic and operational contexts, benefit-cost analysis enables a comparison of the cost efficiencies of different responses.

For projects with SMART objectives, a theory of change, and either an end-of-project review or an impact evaluation (see Minimum Standard 8.6), benefit-cost analysis is straightforward. You will need to know the project costs, including the cost of inputs, such as seeds or tools, and the cost of overheads and technical, logistical, monitoring and evaluation, and support staff. You will also need to estimate a monetary value of the livelihood impacts predicted in the end-of-project review. Because it cannot be based on actual livelihood impacts, a benefit-cost analysis done as part of an end-of-project review will only be indicative.

Benefit-cost analysis also requires a good understanding of non-project costs that contributed to the impacts. For example, the value of any labor, seed, fertilizer, or other inputs provided by crop producers themselves should be calculated and included in the analysis.

Case Study 8.3 (see SEADS website) shows how costs and benefits can be estimated for crop-related projects.

Minimum Standard 8.6: Participatory impact evaluation

Participatory impact evaluation measures livelihood impacts during or at the end of a project.

Key actions

- Compare the project objectives with the actual livelihood impacts that are evident at the end of the project (see Guidance notes 1, 3, and 4).

- Ensure that participatory impact evaluation assesses project contribution (see Guidance note 2).

- Consider the use of benefit-cost analysis to complement participatory impact evaluation (see Guidance note 2 of Minimum Standard 8.5).

Guidance notes

1.　**Participatory impact evaluation.** Participatory impact evaluation of projects is needed where livelihood impacts are expected during a project (or soon after) or to complement an end-of-project review where additional impacts are expected after a project ends. An important advantage of using SMART objectives and a theory of change that both specify livelihood impacts is that the key questions for the evaluation can relate directly to the project objectives, theory of change, and the corresponding indicators. For example, were the project objectives/livelihood impacts achieved and if not, why not? Other questions might examine impacts on specific gender or wealth groups or aim to identify changes to project design that might improve future impacts. A further question might cover the cost efficiency of the project and include a benefit-cost analysis.

2.   **Assessing project contribution.** An impact evaluation should aim to not only measure livelihood impacts, but also to understand how these impacts happened. What were the specific causes of the impacts and the relative importance of these causes? These questions are often captured using the concept of contribution, which assesses a project's contribution to impact relative to non-project factors (ALNAP 2016). For example, a household might need 75 kg of seed but only be able to produce 25 kg of seed (that is, 33% of their needs) themselves. If the balance of 50 kg of seed (that is, 67% of the household's needs) is provided as part of a crop-related crisis response, then the response contributes to 67% of the harvest. Household contribution is often overlooked in impact evaluations. When this or other non-project factors are omitted from evaluations, contribution cannot be fully assessed and project impacts can be inflated.

Using the theory of change in Appendix 8.4 as an example, the project provided seeds and fertilizer but it did not provide other inputs, such as tools, labor, and pest control, that were needed to ensure production. Production also needed the right climatic conditions and secure land access. Market access and reasonable prices were needed to ensure livelihood impacts. While crop producers themselves might have provided tools and pesticide, these inputs might also have been provided by other humanitarian organizations. Therefore, although the theory of change in this case is relatively simple, the assessment of contribution is complex. Understanding the project contribution of crop-related crisis response requires you to:

- Examine the project objectives and theory of change (or logframe), taking account of any changes to implementation that occurred; revise the expected impacts as needed.
- Use simple participatory scoring or proportional piling methods with targeted households to list and score the main factors that are viewed as contributing to the impacts.

Use probing questions to check the technical plausibility of the responses.

3.   **Crop production.** Many crop-related crisis responses will have a theory of change that includes crop production as an output or outcome. Therefore, a measure of crop yields is useful for understanding contribution, while also recognizing that crop production alone is not a livelihood impact. Obtaining the target yield does not automatically mean the expected livelihood impact will be achieved. Commodity prices can fluctuate hugely, losses in crop storage may be

significant, and/or there may be limited access to markets. If you make assumptions about the livelihood impact of a particular yield, test these through discussions with crop producers.

Methods for estimating yields vary in terms of their cost-effectiveness, scale, and accuracy. Select one that fits the context you are operating in and makes the best use of available resources (see Appendix 8.6).

4. **Quantitative impact evaluation.** Quantitative impact evaluation uses evaluation designs and methods that are similar to those that are used in quantitative research. It often uses techniques such as random sampling and sample size estimates using mathematical formulas; this requires specialized technical support. The effectiveness of an intervention is usually based on statistical tests. Quantitative impact evaluation might produce statements such as, "Post-harvest household income was significantly higher for crop producers who received project inputs relative to those who received no inputs, and therefore the project was effective in supporting livelihoods." Quantitative impact evaluation can complement participatory review or impact evaluation, especially if policy makers or senior technical experts prefer to use quantitative research to guide decision making or for advocacy. In humanitarian contexts, it is important that quantitative research approaches be as flexible and participatory as possible, and that assessment and evaluation teams have the required technical expertise to carry them out. Although tools such as mobile apps can speed up data collection in quantitative surveys, to align with SEADS Principle 2 individual surveys should be complemented with other participatory impact and monitoring methods (see Appendix 8.2).

A further challenge with some quantitative impact evaluations of crop-related crisis response relates to the use of randomized control trials. This approach can exclude some people from assistance by using them as a control group. This contradicts the basic principles of humanitarian action as defined by the *Core Humanitarian Standard*. Randomized control trials that take place when assistance is being rolled out in stages or scaled up over seasons can avoid this exclusion.

Recommended reading

Details of references cited in this chapter are in Annex C. Further recommended reading includes:

Byrne, K. (2022). *Applying adaptive management to livelihoods in emergency settings: challenges and opportunities.* Mercy Corps (as part of the Strengthening Capacity in Agriculture, Livelihoods, and Environment (SCALE) Associate Award). https://www.fsnnetwork.org/resource/applying-adaptive-management-livelihoods-emergency-settings-challenges-and-opportunities

Foresti, M. (2003). *A practical guide to assessment, monitoring, review and evaluation.* Save the Children. https://resourcecentre.savethechildren.net/document/practical-guide-assessment-monitoring-review-and-evaluation-2nd-edition/

Global Food Security Cluster (2020). *Food security and livelihoods indicator handbook.* Programme Quality Working Group. https://fscluster.org/page/indicators

Guenet, D. & Uyen, V.N. (2011). *Cost-benefit analysis for interventions supported by the Swiss Agency for Development and Cooperation (SDC) in Vietnam through the PSARD project.* Swiss Agency for Development and Cooperation (SDC).

Inter-Agency Standing Committee (IASC) (2012). *Accountability to affected populations: Tools to assist in implementing the IASC AAP commitments.* https://interagencystandingcommittee.org/system/files/legacy_files/TOOLS%20to%20assist%20in%20implementing%20the%20IASC%20AAP%20Commitments.pdf

Save the Children, International Rescue Committee (IRC) & Mercy Corps (2022). *Multi-purpose cash assistance M&E toolkit.* https://www.fsnnetwork.org/resource/multi-purpose-cash-assistance-mpca-me-toolkit

Sud, U., Ahmad, T., Gupta, V. & Chandra, H. (2017). *Methodology for estimation of crop area and crop yield under mixed and continuous cropping.* Technical report series: GO-21-2017. FAO. https://www.researchgate.net/publication/349075583

Willenbockel, D. (2011). *A cost-benefit analysis of practical action's livelihood-centred disaster risk reduction project in Nepal.* Institute of Development Studies at the University of Sussex, Brighton, UK. http://hdl.handle.net/11283/366214

Appendix 8.1: Examples of livelihood impact indicators for crop-related crisis response

Table A8.1: Examples of livelihood impact indicators for crop-related crisis response

Livelihood asset	Illustrative impact indicators for crop-related crisis responses
Financial	Income derived from the sale of crops per household, relative to total household income. Secondary impact income indicators could focus on the specific uses of income, such as to buy food, crop production supplies, or medicines, or to pay school fees
Natural	Area of land accessed per household relative to baseline (for a response that aims to ensure access or expand crop production land)
Physical	Use of new or rehabilitated infrastructure relative to baseline (for a project aiming to construct or rehabilitate crop-related infrastructure)
Human	Proportion of household dietary energy requirements from own-crop consumption
Social	Strengthening of social networks and collaboration between network members

Livelihood impact indicators are most meaningful if they include a reference point, such as the total amount of a certain crops consumed in a normal year or the total household income required.

For example, for a project that provides rice seed and fertilizer, you might measure:

- average proportion of household rice food needs met relative to a normal year
- average proportion of total household income derived from rice sales
- average uses of income derived from rice sales.

This type of project might produce impacts such as, "On average, project households were able to meet 62% of their rice food (own consumption) needs, and an average of 27% of household income was derived from rice sales. Of this income, 40% of income was spent on agricultural inputs, 40% on food, 10% on school fees, and the remaining 10% on other items."

For a project that aims to rehabilitate a damaged community irrigation scheme, you might measure:

- average area of irrigated land planted relative to the pre-crisis situation
- average proportion of crop-based food needs met per household
- average income from crop sales relative to average household income needs.

This type of project might produce impacts such as, "On average, project households were able to plant 0.3 hectares (ha) relative to pre-crisis cultivation of 0.4 ha. The average income from irrigated crop sales was US$400 relative to annual household income needs of US$5,200."

For projects that aim to support pre-existing systems or services, impact indicators could include:

- number of private sector input sellers at seed fair and average value of vouchers redeemed per seller and type of inputs sold
- partnership with local government extension agents for detecting and controlling crop pests
- use of loans or subsidies to private sector transporters
- use of local tool producers and average value of tools purchased per producer.

ICRC's *Economic Security Indicators Cookbook* provides additional examples (2021).

Appendix 8.2: Participatory methods for monitoring and impact evaluation of crop-related crisis responses

Table A8.2: Examples of participatory methods and illustrative uses for monitoring and impact evaluation of crop-related crisis responses

Participatory method	Illustrative uses	Notes
Interviewing methods		
Individual semi-structured interviews	Can be used to collect information on any topic Information can be quantitative (for example, income from crop sales) or qualitative (for example, security situation during project implementation) Important method for cross-checking and probing information from visualization and scoring methods	Semi-structured approach combines structure with flexibility Cross-check with other methods and process-monitoring data Repetition of interviews that produce quantitative data enables data to be summarized using statistics as needed
Group semi-structured interviews (focus group discussions)	As above	As above
Visualization methods		
Timeline	Timing of responses against crop production cycle	Useful for assessing the timeliness and relevance of project support

...continued

Participatory mapping	Community and land boundaries Areas of land rehabilitated relative to all farming land Areas of land cultivated relative to all farming land	Areas of land cultivated or rehabilitated can be quantified if a scale is applied to maps
Service maps	Before-and-after project access to markets and input sellers	Useful for projects that aim to improve market access or links between producers and sellers
Transect walks	Observations of crop production Observations of use of project-supplied tools Observations of crops managed for pest control	Useful especially when cross-checked with informal interviews
Causal diagrams	Project contribution—visualizing linkages from project and non-project inputs and issues to livelihood impacts	Review findings against project theory of change Linkages can be weighted or scored; repetition of method produces data that can be summarized using statistics as needed
Participatory video and photographs	Recording issues and impacts during a project as selected by community members	Can use photovoice approaches Can be used to compare priorities and perspectives of different social or wealth groups

Ranking and scoring methods		
Proportional piling	Before-and-after proportions of types of household income and changes in total income Before-and-after proportions of food types consumed and changes in total food consumption	Most useful when the method is repeated with different individual informants or groups of informants; results can then be summarized using statistics as needed Cross-check results against theory of change and a review of technical plausibility; support with causal diagrams
Matrix scoring	Comparison of issues and impacts of different responses: • agricultural and non-agricultural • different crop-related responses	Useful for understanding the relative impacts of different responses Findings might be compared with benefit-cost analyses of the responses Repetition enables statistical summaries and analyses as needed

Adapted from Gujit (1998) and Catley et al. (2014)

Appendix 8.3: An example of applying SMART objectives to a crop-related crisis response

An NGO project proposal states the following objective: "Improve the agricultural production of crisis-affected households through provision of seed and other inputs." This objective outlines what the project is trying to achieve but is far too vague to support an assessment of technical plausibility or impact. Although impact indicators could be identified for the objective, it is more efficient to use a SMART objective.

A SMART objective for the same project could be: "In Hamsi district of Amuristan, provide wheat seed and diammonium phosphate and urea fertilizer to 700 vulnerable households so that production covers own consumption and seed needs, and sales contribute to at least 15% of household income in the 2005 post-harvest season." This objective is:

Specific because it states the project area, the type of household to be targeted, and the specific type of seed and fertilizer to provide.

Measurable because it states a quantified target for the income impact (15% of income) and targets for wheat consumption (100%) and wheat seed needs (100%), as identified with focus groups during the response identification.

Achievable because it is based on a participatory initial assessment in which focus groups described sources of crop and non-crop-related income, uses of wheat, and average incomes from wheat sales in a typical year.

Relevant because in the participatory initial assessment, focus groups described the characteristics of more-vulnerable households, the relative importance of different sources of crop- and non-crop-related income, and the relative importance of different crops as sources of income.

Time-bound because it specifies when the livelihood impact will occur and draws on the crop production cycle described by focus groups during the initial assessment.

Appendix 8.4: Example of a simple theory of change for a crop-related crisis response that delivered seeds and fertilizer

This example of a theory of change is from a project in south-central Asia that responded to a complex crisis. A kit of improved certified wheat seeds was provided for each household for irrigated cultivation, along with diammonium phosphate (DAP) fertilizer and urea fertilizer. Different organizations define *outputs*, *outcomes*, and *impacts* differently when using a theory of change, but in this example, agriculture production has been positioned as an outcome.

Figure A8.1: A simple theory of change for a crop-related crisis response that delivered seeds and fertilizer

Inputs	Activity	Output	Outcomes	Impacts
Per household: 50 kg improved wheat seed 50 kg DAP fertilizer 50 kg urea fertilizer	On average, 0.4 ha cultivated with wheat per household with provided kit	Average wheat production per household: 1200 kg	Average uses of wheat crop per household: 600 kg for own consumption 100 kg seed stored 500 kg sold	Household covers own wheat consumption and seed needs, and generates 15% of household income

Assumptions and risks to consider between stages

Inputs/activities to outputs	Outputs to outcomes	Outcomes to impacts
• security conditions enable access to land • minimal consumption of seed • minimal seed or fertilizer sold • correct application of seed and fertilizer • adequate labor • adequate tools	• security conditions enable access to land • adequate rainfall • no substantial pests or diseases • adequate labor • adequate tools • yield from improved seed is about 33% higher than traditional seed • household can decide on the use of the whole production obtained	• peaceful conditions with minimal theft of seed • no grain debts (for example, to landowners) • market or seller access enables seed sales • typical market prices for wheat are maintained • adequate seed storage until consumption or sale

Appendix 8.5: Tracking alignment with SEADS—key process indicators

Table A8.3 provides examples of process indicators that help monitor alignment with SEADS principles and minimum standards. Note that disaggregation of indicators by vulnerability status can help distinguish how key processes may or may not have been appropriate for certain groups.

Table A8.3: Key process indicators to monitor alignment with SEADS principles and minimum standards

No.	Key process indicator	Principles and standards monitored
1	Key response team members trained in use of SEADS	All
2	Key response team members with essential knowledge and skills as in Annex B	All
3	Targeted participants are actively and equitably engaged in assessment, response identification, targeting, implementation, and evaluation of crop-related responses	SEADS Principle 2, Minimum Standards 4.1, 8.1, 8.6

Initial assessment

No.	Key process indicator	Principles and standards monitored
4	Appendixes 4.1, 5.1, 6.1, 7.1 were used to select assessment questions	Minimum Standards 5.1, 6.1, 7.1
5	Technical data were collected at the same time as initial assessment data where possible	Minimum Standards 4.2, 4.3, 5.1, 6.1, 7.1
6	Initial assessment is completed in a participatory manner and written report(s), in appropriate local language(s), is/are available to team members	Minimum Standards 4.1, 5.1, 6.1, 7.1
7	Acute constraints to crop production have been identified and links have been made with development programs to address chronic constraints	Minimum Standards 5.1, 6.1, 7.1
8	Approach to data collection draws on existing secondary data and information	Minimum Standards 4.2, 4.3

9	Initial assessment and technical data from different sources cross-checked for consistency	Minimum Standards 4.1, 4.2
10	Initial assessment determined that a crop-related response is or is not appropriate, necessary, and feasible	SEADS Principle 1, Minimum Standard 4.2
11	Criteria of selection for targeting the most in need are defined and relevant to the context	Minimum Standard 4.3
12	Different targeting methods are considered and the most suitable identified	Minimum Standard 4.3
13	Where livestock play a critical role in livelihoods alongside crop production, Livestock Emergency Guidelines and Standards Chapter 3: Initial Assessment and Identifying Responses was used to inform initial assessment	SEADS Principles 1 and 5, Minimum Standard 4.3

Response identification

14	SEADS livelihood objectives and their relevance to the context are understood	SEADS Principle 1, Minimum Standards 4.4, 5.2, 6.2, 7.2, 8.2, 8.4
15	A participatory RAIT is complete and potential response areas identified	Minimum Standard 4.4
16	Scoring of the RAIT was based on initial assessment and technical data and consensus of participants	SEADS Principles 1 and 2, Minimum Standard 4.4
17	Decision tree results identifying appropriate technical options and related minimum standards are available and show links between assessment results and technical options selected	Minimum Standards 4.4, 5.2, 6.2, 7.2

...continued

18	Market-based responses have been considered and favored where possible	SEADS Principle 1, Minimum Standards 5.2, 6.2, 7.1
19	Timeline(s) with potential delivery bottlenecks relative to critical seasonal tasks for all technical options identified	Minimum Standards 5.2, 6.2, 7.3
20	Quality criteria for seed, tools, equipment, and other non-seed inputs were established that were at least as good as crop producers routinely used, and were acceptable to farming communities, donors, authorities, and practitioners	Minimum Standards 5.5, 6.5
21	Quality and technical specifications verification throughout the response timed to reject bad-quality seed, tools, equipment, other non-seed inputs or infrastructure, if needed	Minimum Standards 5.5, 6.5, 7.3
22	Crop-related responses are coordinated with other actors delivering responses in the target area	SEADS Principle 5
23	Crop-related responses include activities to ensure environmental protection	SEADS Principle 4, Minimum Standard 7.2
24	Calculations of the scale of assistance are based on appropriate targeting, real-time costs, sowing rates, access to assets, and appropriate and safe delivery mechanisms	Minimum Standards 5.2, 6.3
25	Written timeline showing consideration of sowing season and bottlenecks	SEADS Principle 1, Minimum Standards 4.2, 5.2, 6.2, 7.3

| 26 | A participatory assessment identifies the key infrastructure rehabilitation needs, the technical requirements, and the location, lifetime, and timing for implementing the rehabilitation, including:

• understanding inequalities in ownership, access, and who would benefit most (security of tenure)
• local legislation, preferred construction techniques, building codes
• positive and negative environmental impacts
• risk mapping
• how to build back better | SEADS Principles 1, 2, Minimum Standard 7.1 |

Implementation of SEADS response areas

27	Data on market prices and crop producers' buying power is available	SEADS Principle 1, Minimum Standards 5.3, 6.3
28	Local and existing seed, tools, equipment, and other non-seed input sources and systems leveraged	SEADS Principle 1, Minimum Standards 5.3, 6.3
29	All seed, tools, equipment, other non-seed inputs, and infrastructure used in a crop-related response: • were known, tried, and tested in the area (varieties, types) • were acceptable to all participants (choice, quality, amounts) • met different requirements and regulations of donors and governments (certifications, planning and building codes) • perform well under crop producers' realistic management conditions	SEADS Principle 1, Minimum Standards 5.4, 5.5, 6.4, 6.5

...continued

- were tailored to the needs and capacities of different crop producers

30	Consideration of crop producer choice, limits, and final recommendations documented	Minimum Standards 5.4, 6.4, 7.2
31	Seed treatment and labeling associated with all inputs were assessed and completed as needed	Minimum Standards 5.4, 5.5, 6.4, 6.5
32	Safety training delivered as required to protect participants	Minimum Standard 6.4
33	Crop-related infrastructure is rehabilitated according to agreed safe practices for the specific context and hazards	Minimum Standards 7.2, 7.3
35	Target participants report the seed, tools, equipment, other non-seed inputs, or infrastructure was functional and accessible and safe when it was needed (disaggregated by in kind or cash and delivery mechanism)	SEADS Principle 1, Minimum Standards 5.2, 6.2, 7.2, 7.3

Monitoring and impact evaluation

36	Project objectives are specific, measurable, achievable, relevant, and time-bound (SMART)	Minimum Standard 8.2
37	A theory of change or logical framework exists for the project and includes SMART objectives, and risks and assumptions	Minimum Standard 8.2
38	Process monitoring was done and real-time adjustments made as needed. The RAIT, the decision trees, and the theory of change were updated as needed	Minimum Standard 8.3
39	Impact indicators directly show meaningful impacts on households	Minimum Standard 8.4

40	If livelihood impacts are expected months after a project ends, a participatory end-of-project review was completed and benefit-cost analysis considered	Minimum Standard 8.5
41	If livelihood impacts are expected at the end of the project, a participatory impact evaluation was completed	Minimum Standard 8.6
42	Rationale for the choice of evaluation is available	Minimum Standards 8.5, 8.6

Appendix 8.6: Methods for estimating crop yields

Table A8.4: Cost-effectiveness, scale, and accuracy in estimation, errors, and biases of methods for estimating crop yields

Method	Cost-effectiveness	Scale	Accuracy in estimation, errors, and biases
Crop cut	Time and labor intensive	Field, farm, and sometimes landscape level	Tendency to overestimate
Farmer's estimate	Cheap and quick method that saves time and money	Farm to landscape	Fairly accurate estimation, but needs adequate supervision Subjective
Sampling harvest unit	Cost-effective	Farm to landscape	Error prone in the condition where crop producers harvest from multiple areas at a time and not possible with staggered harvesting

...continued

Whole plot harvest	Cost and labor intensive	Plot level, farm level, case study	Almost bias/error-free
Expert assessment	Moderately cost-effective	From farm to landscape level	Chance of error increases if different teams of experts are used or extension people are used to estimate yield in their own area Subjective
Crop cards	Cost and labor intensive	Field to farm level	Bias due to illiteracy, use of local units, etc.
Crop modeling	Cost-effective	Landscape	More accurate if adequately parameterized and calibrated. Does not include induced improvements in agricultural technology
Purchaser's/ insurance record	Cost-effective	Field scale	Suitable for cash crops only with no household consumption
Allometric models	Cost-effective	Field scale	Suitable for few crops
Remote sensing	Cost-effective	Landscape	Chance of error in cases where different crops have the same signature

Adapted from Sapkota et al. (2016)

ANNEXES

Annex A: Glossary

Agricultural inputs	The resources that are used in farm production, such as chemicals, equipment, feed, and seed. Also referred to simply as *inputs*.
Alarm	The second phase of a slow-onset crisis.
Alert	The first phase of a slow-onset crisis.
Anticipatory action	Short-term crisis risk management responses that are implemented after it is known that a crisis is likely to occur but before it actually occurs. These actions aim to prevent and/or mitigate the impact of the crisis on vulnerable households.
Assets	A resource of value. Includes *livelihood assets*, *permanent assets*, and *productive assets*.
Build back better	The use of the recovery, rehabilitation, and reconstruction phases after a crisis to increase the resilience of communities and households through integrating disaster risk reduction measures into the restoration of physical infrastructure and societal systems, and into the revitalization of livelihoods, economies, and the environment (United Nations General Assembly 2016).
Cash and voucher assistance	Cash or vouchers are provided, either physically or via remote transfer, to give the recipient crop producers purchasing power.
Cash for work	A form of conditional cash payment, whereby eligible people are required to complete specified public or community work programs before receiving a cash payment. Typically used when an organization wishes to directly support people and repair or rehabilitate permanent assets and/or natural resources.
Cash grant	Provision of cash without restriction on its use. Also referred to as unconditional cash or cash relief.

Certified seed	Seed of a known variety produced under strict, formally regulated standards to maintain varietal purity and high degrees of seed health. Seed lots must also be free of inert matter and weed seeds. All certified seed must pass field inspection, be conditioned by an approved seed conditioning plant, and then be sampled and pass laboratory testing before it can be sold as certified seed.
Chronic emergency	A crisis in which the phases (alert, alarm, emergency, recovery) keep repeating themselves without returning to normal.
Complex emergency	A humanitarian crisis in a country, region, or society where there is total or considerable breakdown of authority resulting from internal or external conflict and which requires an international response that goes beyond the mandate or capacity of any single organization and/or the ongoing United Nations country program (IASC 1994).
Crisis response	A set of actions and decisions taken before, during, and after a crisis that together make up the response. SEADS notably includes preparedness and anticipatory action as part of crisis response and has three response areas: seed and seed systems; tools, equipment, and other non-seed inputs; and crop-related infrastructure.
Crop	A cultivated annual, perennial, or horticulture plant that is grown as food.
Crop producer	Anyone who produces food from annual, perennial, or horticulture crops for consumption or income. SEADS livelihood objectives focus on those who rely on crop production for their livelihoods although they may also do other income-generating activities, such as livestock production.
Delivery mechanism	Means by which cash assistance is distributed to targeted participants, such as vouchers, cash, or mobile money.
Direct seed distribution (DSD)	A crisis response in which seed is procured for and delivered to crop producers because seed is unavailable locally. It is the most widely used response to seed availability constraints.

Disaster risk reduction (DRR)	Efforts to prevent new and reduce existing disaster risk through the implementation of integrated and inclusive economic, structural, legal, social, health, cultural, educational, environmental, technological, political, and institutional measures that prevent and reduce hazard exposure and vulnerability to disaster, increase preparedness for response and recovery, and thus strengthen resilience (United Nations Office for Disaster Risk Reduction 2015).
Early recovery	The second phase of a rapid-onset crisis. It is a set of specific responses to help affected people move from humanitarian support toward self-sustaining development. It encompasses the restoration of basic services, livelihoods, shelter, governance, security and rule of law, environment, and social dimensions, including the reintegration of displaced populations.
Emergency	The third phase of a slow-onset crisis.
Evaluation	A comprehensive, usually formal, assessment of a project. Typically, it relates project activities and achievements of project objectives, so the value of an evaluation depends partly on the clarity and relevance of the stated project objectives. Evaluation can also assess the efficiency of work in relation to resources, particularly financial inputs, and can look at the sustainability and long-term implications of projects. Evaluations usually take place at the end of projects.
Exclusion error	An error in targeting that results in people who should be included in a response (because they meet the criteria) not being included.
Formal seed system	Production and supply of seed of modern varieties and certified seed through an organized chain, including specialized plant breeders, regulated seed producers, specialized commercial outlets, or government extension agencies. It always includes the process of certification.

Hybrid	The first-generation seed of a cross between two different parent seeds, which often displays special vigor. The seed cannot be replanted with the same expected performance. To maintain vigor, hybrid seed has to be rebought every planting season.
Immediate aftermath	The first phase of a rapid-onset crisis; the period just after the crisis, when the impact is greatest.
Impact evaluation	Looks at a project's effects on people, the environment, or institutions. It identifies the changes that have occurred in people's livelihoods during a project and determines whether and how these changes relate to project activities. Humanitarian and development organizations often refer to the link between project activities and impact as "contribution" or "attribution," which is similar to the more scientific terms "association" or "causation."
Impact indicator	Point of reference for measuring the result of actions taken in terms of their effect on people's livelihoods (LEGS Glossary).
Inclusion error	An error in targeting that results in people being included in the response who should not be because they do not meet the criteria.
Indicators	Measurements (either qualitative or quantitative) of the progress of a response; they are divided into process indicators and impact indicators.
Informal seed system	Seed obtained from crop producers' own harvests and social networks, and selected from local markets. These seed systems, which can diffuse local or modern varieties (which are recycled), tend to be governed by local norms of practice rather than official or government standards. Seed is not backed by formal certification.
Initial assessment	The collection and analysis of initial information about the role that crops play in livelihoods, about the nature and impact of the emergency, and a situation analysis (LEGS Glossary).

Integrated pest management	The careful consideration of all available pest control techniques and subsequent integration of appropriate measures that discourage the development of pest populations. It emphasizes the growth of healthy crops with the least possible disruption to agro-ecosystems and encourages natural pest control mechanisms (FAO 2022).
Integrated seed system	Combination of different aspects of the formal and informal seed supply systems. An example is a community-based seed group that gets outside technical support.
Key action	Key step or measure that contributes to achieving the *standard*.
Livelihood	The capabilities, assets (including both material and non-material resources), and activities required to make a living.
Livelihood assets	The resources, equipment, skills, strengths, and relationships that are used by individuals and households to pursue their livelihoods; they are categorized as social, human, natural, financial, and physical and form part of the livelihoods framework (LEGS Glossary).
Livelihoods framework	A model showing how individuals and households use their different assets and livelihood strategies to make a living but are also affected by their own vulnerabilities and the policy and institutional context in which they work (LEGS Glossary).
Livelihood impact	Impacts that affect targeted participant livelihood assets. See *Livelihood assets* and Appendix 8.1.
Livelihood objective	The purpose for which a crop-related response is undertaken in SEADS. Generally, this is to improve long-term livelihood security and quality of life. SEADS promotes three livelihood objectives:

1. to provide immediate livelihood benefits to crop-producing households affected by crisis.
2. to protect crop-related livelihoods of households affected by crisis.

3. to rebuild or support crop-related production, infrastructure, and systems to ensure livelihoods for households affected by crisis.

Market	An organized exchange between buyers and sellers of goods and services.
Market system	A multiplayer, multilocation, and multifunction arrangement that allows or influences the functioning of a specific good/service market. A market system has three main parts: the core (the market chain), the environment (law and regulations), and the support structure (services and infrastructure).
Modern variety	A seed variety developed by formal plant breeders that is distinct, uniform, and stable. The term is sometimes used interchangeably with the terms "high-yielding variety" and "improved variety" but in performance may not necessarily have these characteristics, especially when used under actual farming conditions.
Monitoring	The systematic measurement of a project over time. It usually involves the regular collection of information. It allows changes to be made during the project, while also providing information for periodic reviews, impact assessments, or evaluations.
Participatory approach	Approaches in which the people implementing the response and the participants in the response work together to understand the situation and change it for the better. These approaches are flexible, can be adapted to local conditions, and acknowledge local people as experts by emphasizing their involvement in planning for projects and assessing project impact.
Permanent assets	Assets that support farming households that cannot be easily transported away from a location without dismantling or deconstructing them. This includes buildings, irrigation works, roads or tracks, and fencing.
Process indicator	A measure of the progress of response activities or what is being done. Examples of process indicators to measure alignment with SEADS are listed in Appendix 8.5.

Productive assets	Items that crop producers use to produce the crops they grow to eat or sell. These assets include cash, seed, machinery and equipment, buildings, and land.
Rapid-onset crisis	A crisis such as an earthquake, flood, or tsunami that hits suddenly and sometimes without warning. It is normally divided into three key phases: immediate aftermath; early recovery; and recovery (LEGS Glossary).
Recovery	The last phase of a slow-onset and rapid-onset crisis. The goal of the recovery phase is to bring the area back to normalcy.
Response	A sum of decisions and actions taken before, during, and after a crisis, including preparedness, immediate relief, early recovery, and rehabilitation. SEADS recognizes three response areas: seed and seed systems; tools, equipment, and other non-seed inputs; and crop-related infrastructure.
Review	An assessment of a project at a specific point in time. It can focus on particular aspects of the project, and involves a more detailed analysis of issues than is possible with monitoring alone. A review is often conducted in response to a specific issue or problem that has arisen. An end-of-project review might be used when sufficient time or resources are not available for an evaluation, or if project objectives or impacts are not expected to be achieved at the end of the project.
Seed	Anything used as planting material. It may be in the form of a grain or a part of a plant (stem, vine, sucker, tuber).
Seed fair	An organized market where crop producers use vouchers distributed by aid organizations to procure seed from sellers, who may be other crop producers, sellers, or formal sector representatives (from government seed agencies or private companies).
Seed quality	The potential performance of a seed lot, which is determined by three attributes: physical qualities of the seed in the specific seed lot; physiological qualities, which refer to aspects of performance of the seed; and seed health, which refers to the presence or absence of diseases and pests within a seed sample.

Seed security	Seed security exists when men and women within the household have sufficient access to adequate quantities of good-quality seed and planting materials of preferred crop varieties at all times in both good and bad cropping seasons (FAO 2016).
Seed security assessment (SSA)	An assessment that examines all the seed channels crop producers might use. It focuses on the supply and demand side and determines if there are constraints in seed availability, access, or quality. The assessment is used to determine if a seed-related intervention is needed.
Seed system	See *formal seed system* and *informal seed system*.
Self (or open-pollinated) variety	Reproduction type in crops that will "breed true." When sown, the seeds will produce plants roughly identical to their parents. Some crops in this category include beans, groundnuts, wheat, and sorghum.
Slow-onset crisis	A crisis, such as a drought or extreme cold season, whose effects are felt gradually. It is normally divided into four phases: alert, alarm, emergency, and recovery (LEGS 2014).
Standard	A qualitative statement applicable in any crisis context that defines minimum actions and outcomes to achieve.
Technical option	An action (done as part of a crisis response) that seeks to address identified production constraints and achieve one or more SEADS livelihood objectives. Each SEADS response is divided into different technical options, which present different ways of delivering a response (for example, facilitate seed access versus support the seed system).
Theory of change	A comprehensive description and illustration of how and why a desired change is expected to happen in a particular context. It is focused on mapping out how program inputs and activities are expected to lead to desired outputs, outcomes, and impact. A theory of change is created by first identifying the desired long-term goals and then working back from these to identify all the conditions (outcomes) that must be in place (and how these relate to one another causally) for the impact to be achieved.

Value-chain actors	Private sector, civil society, and state actors who produce and sell goods and services in the crop-related value-chain, such as transporters, seed producers, extension agents, and input dealers.
Vegetatively propagated crops	Reproduction type whereby a new plant grows from a fragment of the parent plant or grows from a specialized reproductive structure (or cutting), such as a tuber, stem, or vine. Some crops in this category include cassava, sweet potato, and bananas.

Annex B: Elements of Team Competency

If key response team members (managers, grant writers, and technical advisors) have crop-related knowledge, experience shows crop-related responses will be more likely to be relevant, appropriate, and have no negative effects. Depending on the technical knowledge of the organization's full-time staff, additional part-time specialists (such as agronomists and engineers) could also be included.

Assess competencies

During preparedness for future hazards, organizations can assess local and international partners' capacities to plan and implement crop-related responses that will be able to achieve SEADS minimum standards and have livelihood impacts. Table C.1 describes the relative desirability of various technical qualifications required for the response areas in SEADS minimum standards. It can be used to develop assessments, write job descriptions, and advocate to donors.

Strengthen competencies

While most international NGOs have a robust capacity-strengthening component for their own staff, the Grand Bargain Localization Workstream (2020) has highlighted the importance of an equal emphasis on strengthening and sharing the capacity of local actors. Ideally, international actors and donors include and allow budget line(s) for these responses in all projects and partnership agreements. Local actors should commit time and other resources to invest in their own capacity and organizational development during normal (non-crisis) periods.

It is best to build staff skills during preparedness or as a crisis context is normalizing. Organizations should strive to achieve the skills in Table B.1 over time. When an organization does not have the necessary in-house expertise for a particular response, it should seek assistance from other organizations (see *Core Humanitarian Standard 6: Coordination*). The specific profile and skill set of the technical staff will depend on the type of response.

Table B.1: Achievement of SEADS minimum standards requires a range of knowledgeable team members

Knowledge area or skill	Minimum standards				
	Initial assessment and response-area identification	Seed and seed systems	Tools, equipment, and other non-seed inputs	Crop-related infrastructure	Impact-oriented monitoring and evaluation
Humanitarian standards, in particular *LEGS, MERS,* and *MISMA*	Essential				
Livelihoods- and rights-based and participatory approaches	Essential				
Vulnerability mainstreaming (see *HIS Standards*)	Essential				
Logistics/ planning (see ULS 2021)	Essential				

Local agricultural context	Desired	Essential	Desired	Desired	Not needed
Private sector engagement	Not needed	Essential	Essential	Essential for communal rehabili-tation (otherwise not needed)	Not needed
Assessments: market and seed security	Essential	Essential	Essential	Desired	Not needed
Market and price monitoring	Desired	Essential	Essential	Desired	Essential
Agronomy	Local expertise desired	Essential	Desired	Essential	Local expertise desired
Agricultural or water engineering	Desired	Not needed	Not needed	Essential	Not needed

Annex C: References

Chapter 1: How to Use this Handbook

Food and Agricultural Organization of the United Nations (FAO) (2021). *Fisheries and aquaculture international guidelines*. FAO. https://www.fao.org/fishery/en/code/guidelines

Sphere Association (2018). *The Sphere handbook: Humanitarian charter and minimum standards in humanitarian response*. Practical Action Publishing. https://handbook.spherestandards.org/en/sphere/#ch001

Chapter 2: The Scope and Approach of SEADS

Age and Disability Capacity Programme (2018). *Humanitarian inclusion standards for older people and people with disabilities.* https://www.hi-us.org/humanitarian_inclusion_standards_for_older_people

The Alliance for Child Protection in Humanitarian Action (2020). *Minimum standards for child protection in humanitarian action.* https://alliancecpha.org/sites/default/files/technical/attachments/cpms_2019_final_en.pdf

Camp Management Standards Working Group (2021). *Minimum standards for camp management.* https://cccmcluster.org/resources/minimum-standards-camp-management

Committee on World Food Security (CFS) (2015). *Framework for action for food security and nutrition in protracted crises.* CFS. http://www.fao.org/fileadmin/templates/cfs/Docs1415/FFA/CFS_FFA_Final_Draft_Ver2_EN.pdf

FAO (2017). *The Impact of disasters and crises on agriculture and food security: 2017.* FAO. https://www.fao.org/3/I8656EN/i8656en.pdf

FAO (2021). *The impact of disasters and crises on agriculture and food security: 2021.* FAO. http://www.fao.org/3/cb3673en/cb3673en.pdf

FAO Data Lab (2021). *Daily food prices acceleration monitor.* FAO. http://www.fao.org/datalab/website/web/food-prices

Implementer-Led Evaluation and Learning (IMPEL) (2022). *Study of the impacts of COVID-19 and other recent shocks in Haiti (Vol. I).* IMPEL Associate Award. https://pdf.usaid.gov/pdf_docs/PA00Z9SD.pdf

Inter-agency Network for Education in Emergencies (2010). *Minimum standards for education: Preparedness, response, recovery.* https://inee.org/minimum-standards

Livestock Emergency Guidelines and Standards (LEGS) Project (2014). *Livestock emergency guidelines and standards* (2nd edn). Practical Action Publishing. http://dx.doi.org/10.3362/9781780448602

OCHA (2020). *Global humanitarian response plan: COVID-19.* United Nations Coordinated Appeal April–December 2020, July update. OCHA. https://www.unocha.org/publication/global-humanitarian-response-plan/global-humanitarian-response-plan-covid-19-july-0

Pelly, I. & Juillard, H. (2018). *Minimum standard for market analysis (MISMA)*. CaLP Network. https://www.calpnetwork.org/publication/minimum-standard-for-market-analysis-misma/

SEADS (2021). *Emergency agriculture interventions: Reviewing evidence on the impacts on livelihoods, food security and nutrition*. https://seads-standards.org/wp-content/uploads/2021/04/SEADS_brief1_4.26.21.pdf

SEEP Network (2017). *Minimum economic recovery standards* (3rd edn). Practical Action Publishing. https://doi.org/10.3362/9781780446707

Sphere Association (2018). *The Sphere handbook: Humanitarian charter and minimum standards in humanitarian response*. Practical Action Publishing. https://handbook.spherestandards.org/en/sphere/#ch001

Tschunkert, K. & Delgado, C. (2022). *Food systems in conflict and peacebuilding settings: Ways forward*. Stockholm International Peace Research Institute. https://www.sipri.org/publications/2022/other-publications/food-systems-conflict-and-peacebuilding-settings-ways-forward

World Bank (2016). *Who are the poor in the developing world?* Poverty and Shared Prosperity Report 2016: Taking on Inequality. Background Paper. https://documents1.worldbank.org/curated/en/187011475416542282/pdf/WPS7844.pdf

World Bank (2021, 15 April). *Poverty: Overview – context* [webpage]. https://www.worldbank.org/en/topic/poverty/overview

Chapter 3: SEADS Principles

FAO (2022). *Climate smart agriculture sourcebook*. FAO. https://www.fao.org/climate-smart-agriculture-sourcebook/en/

Forcier Consulting Sudan (2017). *Darfur community peace and stability fund phase II evaluation*. Darfur Community Peace & Stability Fund. https://seads-standards.org/wp-content/uploads/2021/04/Forcier-Consulting-Sudan-2017.pdf

International Committee of the Red Cross (ICRC) (2019). *EcoSec project review report: ILOT – Rehabilitation of agricultural lands in the border area (100–300 m) from the security fence*. Summary report. ICRC. https://seads-standards.org/wp-content/uploads/2021/05/Asia_03-ICRC-Approved-Summary-Review-report-ILOT-Land-rehabilitation.pdf

Jones, C., Guerten, N., Hillesland, M. & Koechlein, E. (2020) *Applying an inclusive and equitable approach to anticipatory action*. FAO. https://www.fao.org/publications/card/en/c/CB1072EN/

Livestock Emergency Guidelines and Standards (LEGS) Project (2014). *Livestock emergency guidelines and standards* (2nd edn). Practical Action Publishing. http://doi.org/10.3362/9781780448602

Momoh, H. & Browne, A. (2019). *Terminal evaluation of strengthening conflict prevention through establishing of multi-stakeholder platforms and improved alternative livelihoods for concession affected communities project*. UN Development Program & FAO. https://seads-standards.org/wp-content/uploads/2021/04/Momoh-and-Browne-2019.pdf

Norwegian Refugee Council (NRC) (2021). *Demystifying "tenure" for humanitarian practitioners*. NRC. https://www.globalprotectioncluster.org/wp-content/uploads/Demystifying-Tenure-for-Humanitarian-Practitioners-2021.pdf

Scoones, I. (1998). *Sustainable rural livelihoods: A framework for analysis*. IDS Working Paper 72. Institute for Development Studies, University of Sussex. https://opendocs.ids.ac.uk/opendocs/bitstream/handle/20.500.12413/3390/Wp72.pdf?sequence=1

SEADS (2021). *Emergency agriculture interventions: Reviewing evidence on the impacts on livelihoods, food security, and nutrition*. https://seads-standards.org/wp-content/uploads/2021/04/SEADS_brief1_4.26.21.pdf

UNEP/OCHA Joint Environment Unit (2021). *Nexus environmental assessment tool (NEAT+)*. https://resources.eecentre.org/resources/neat/

World Wildlife Fund (WWF) (2017). *Green recovery and reconstruction: Training toolkit for humanitarian aid (GRRT)*. WWF & American Red Cross. https://files.worldwildlife.org/wwfcmsprod/files/Publication/file/6yv8ayzl1y_Combined_GRRT.pdf?_ga=2.71116373.478864359.1636482104-1642110664.1634207796

Chapter 4: Initial Assessment for Crop-related Crisis Response

Albu, M. (2010). Emergency market mapping and analysis toolkit. Practical Action Publishing. https://www.emma-toolkit.org/toolkit

ALNAP (2021). *Targeting for improved humanitarian response portal* [website]. UNHCR. https://targeting.alnap.org/

Global Food Security Cluster (2022). *Farmers' engagement survey*. Agriculture Working Group. https://fscluster.org/sites/default/files/documents/farmer_ engagement_survey_report_final_draft_rev.pdf

IRC (2016). *Revised pre-crisis market analysis*. International Rescue Committee. https://www.emma-toolkit.org/pre-crisis

Schoonmaker Freudenberger, K. (2008). *Rapid rural appraisal (RRA) and participatory rural appraisal (PRA): A manual for CRS field workers and partners*. Catholic Relief Services (CRS). https://www.crs.org/sites/default/files/tools-research/rapid-rural-appraisal-and-participatory-rural-appraisal.pdf

Stewart, S. (1998). *Learning together: The agricultural worker's participatory sourcebook*. Heifer Project International.

Chapter 5: Seed and Seed Systems

Albu, M. (2010). *Emergency market mapping and analysis toolkit*. Practical Action Publishing. https://www.emma-toolkit.org/toolkit

Bramel, P.J., Nagoda, S., Haugen, J.M., Adugna, D., Dejene, T., Bekel, T. & Traedal, L.T. (2004). Relief seed assistance in Ethiopia. In L. Sperling, T. Remington, J.M. Haugen & S. Nagoda (eds.), *Addressing seed security in disaster response: Linking relief with development* (pp. 111–134). https://hdl.handle.net/10568/103352

Cullis, A. (2020). *An impact assessment of permagardens in Palabek refugee settlement, northern Uganda*. African Women Rising. https://www.africanwomenrising.org/wp-content/uploads/2020/04/AWR-Permagarden-PIA-2019-FINAL.pdf

FAO (2010a). *Quality declared planting material: Protocols and standards for vegetatively propagated crops*. Plant Production and Protection Paper 195. FAO. http://www.fao.org/3/i1195e/i1195e.pdf

FAO (2010b). *Seeds in emergencies: A technical handbook*. Plant Production and Protection Paper 202. FAO. https://www.fao.org/publications/card/en/c/0c46c45f-eeec-5dcb-8c22-519f116297d1/

FAO (2012a). *Kharif 2011 intervention report. Post harvest survey and effects of the 2011 floods in Sindh Province: Part of FAO's flood response Pakistan*. Unpublished. FAO.

FAO (2012b). *Post harvest survey report, Zaid Rabi 2011/12 agricultural interventions under projects OSRO/PAK/107/AUL and OSRO/PAK/109/UK, part of FAO's flood response in Pakistan.* Unpublished. FAO.

FAO (2015). *Voluntary guide for national seed policy formulation.* FAO. https://www.fao.org/plant-treaty/tools/toolbox-for-sustainable-use/details/en/c/1071260/

FAO (2016). *Seed security assessment: A practitioner's guide.* FAO. https://www.fao.org/plant-treaty/tools/toolbox-for-sustainable-use/details/en/c/1071289/

FAO, SeedSystem & USAID/OFDA (2020). *Minimum technical standards for seed system assessment (SSA) in emergencies.* https://fscluster.org/sites/default/files/documents/minimum-seed-systems-standards-final-.pdf

Haugen, J.M. & Fowler, C. (2003). Re-assessing the need for emergency seed relief post-disaster: The case of Honduras after Hurricane Mitch. *The Journal of Humanitarian Assistance.*

Henderson, R. & Herby, L. (2019). *Ditekemena emergency food security project evaluation September to October 2019.* CRS, Democratic Republic of Congo. https://seads-standards.org/wp-content/uploads/2021/04/Henderson-R-2019.pdf

International Seed Testing Association (ISTA) (2022). *International rules for seed testing* [webpage]. ISTA. https://www.seedtest.org/en/publications/international-rules-seed-testing-1168.html

McGuire, S. & Sperling, L. (2013). Making seed systems more resilient to stress. *Global Environmental Change 23,* 644–653. https://doi.org/10.1016/j.gloenvcha.2013.02.001

Mollet, M. (2010). *Report on outputs and outcomes obtained by the project; Emergency provision of agricultural inputs and support to agriculture sector and food security cluster coordination in Georgia.* FAO. Unpublished.

Pincus, L., Dubois, T., Marks, P. & Sperling, L. (2017). *Emergency vegetable seed interventions: Can we expect improved nutrition or income generation among beneficiaries?* CRS. https://seedsystem.org/wp-content/uploads/2017/05/Emergency-Vegetable-Seed-Interventions-final.pdf

Pretari, A. & Anguko, A. (2019). *Livelihoods in South Sudan: Impact evaluation of the "South Sudan Peace and Prosperity Promotion" project.* Effectiveness Review Series 2016/17. Oxfam GB. https://seads-standards.org/wp-content/uploads/2021/04/Pretari-2019.pdf

Remington, T., Maroko, J., Walsh, S., Omanga, P. & Charles, E. (2002). Getting off the seeds-and-tools treadmill with CRS seed vouchers and fairs. *Disasters 26*, 316–328. https://doi.org/10.1111/1467-7717.00209

Rohrbach, D.D., Mashingaidze, A.B. & Mudhara, M. (2005). *Distribution of relief seed and fertilizer in Zimbabwe: Lessons from the 2003/04 season.* International Crops Research Institute for the Semi-arid Tropics (ICRISAT) and FAO. Unpublished.

SEADS (2021). *Emergency agriculture interventions: Reviewing evidence on the impacts on livelihoods, food security and nutrition.* https://seads-standards.org/wp-content/uploads/2021/04/SEADS_brief1_4.26.21.pdf

Sperling, L., Cooper, H. & Remington, T. (2008). Moving towards more effective seed aid. *Journal of Development Studies 44*, 586–612. https://doi.org/10.1080/00220380801980954

Sperling, L., Gallagher, P., McGuire, S., March, J. & Templer, N. (2020). Informal seed traders: The backbone of seed business and African smallholder seed supply. *Sustainability 12*, 7074. https://doi.org/10.3390/su12177074

Sperling, L., Mottram, A., Ouko, W. & Love, A. (2022). *Seed emergency response tool: Guidance for practitioners.* Produced by Mercy Corps and SeedSystem as a part of the ISSD Africa activity. https://issdafrica.org/wp-content/uploads/2022/06/SERT_Digital_Jun22.pdf

Van Duivenbooden, N., Pala, M., Studer, C., Bielders, C.L. & Beukes, D.J. (2000). Cropping systems and crop complementarity in dryland agriculture to increase soil water use efficiency: A review. *NJAS: Wageningen Journal of Life Sciences 48*, 213–236. https://doi.org/10.1016/S1573-5214(00)80015-9

Waha, K., Müller, C., Bondeau, A., Dietrich, J.P., Kurukulasuriya, P., Heinke, J. & Lotze-Campen, H. (2013). Adaptation to climate change through the choice of cropping system and sowing date in sub-Saharan Africa. *Global Environmental Change 23*, 130–143. https://doi.org/10.1016/j.gloenvcha.2012.11.001

Weatherall, J. (2019). *After action review (AAR): Agricultural recovery and resilience project (ARRP).* CRS. Unpublished.

World Bank (2012). *Implementation completion and results report for a Zimbabwe emergency agricultural input project*. https://seads-standards.org/wp-content/uploads/2021/04/World-Bank-2012-Zimbabwe.pdf

Chapter 6: Tools, Equipment, and Other Non-seed Inputs

Agriculture Knowledge, Learning, Documentation and Policy (AKLDP) Project (2016). *El Niño in Ethiopia: Early impacts of drought in Amhara National Regional State*. Field notes. https://agri-learning-ethiopia.org/wp-content/uploads/2016/01/AKLDP-Field-Notes-Amhara-Jan-2016.pdf

Albu, M. (2010). *Emergency market mapping and analysis toolkit*. Practical Action Publishing. https://www.emma-toolkit.org/toolkit

Cronin, D. (2020, 11 November). Farm tools designed for men pose problems for female farmers. *Harvest Public Media*. https://givingcompass.org/article/farm-tools-designed-for-men-pose-problems-for-female-farmers/

Cullis, A. (2020). *An impact assessment of permagardens in Palabek refugee settlement, northern Uganda*. African Women Rising. https://www.africanwomenrising.org/wp-content/uploads/2020/04/AWR-Permagarden-PIA-2019-FINAL.pdf

FAO (2012a). *Kharif 2011 intervention report. Post harvest survey and effects of the 2011 floods in Sindh Province: Part of FAO's flood response Pakistan*. Unpublished. FAO.

FAO (2012b). *Post harvest survey report, Zaid Rabi 2011/12 agricultural interventions under projects OSRO/PAK/107/AUL and OSRO/PAK/109/UK, part of FAO's flood response in Pakistan*. Unpublished. FAO.

FAO (2021). *Crop calendar – information tool for crop production*. FAO. https://cropcalendar.apps.fao.org/#/

Millican, J., Perkins, C. & Adam-Bradford, A. (2019). Gardening in displacement: The benefits of cultivating in crisis. *Journal of Refugee Studies 32*, 351–371. https://doi.org/10.1093/jrs/fey033

Mollet, M. (2009). *Emergency support for the restoration of food security in the areas of southern Myanmar affected by Cyclone Nargis: Beneficiaries results assessment (BRA) survey*. Unpublished. FAO.

Pajot, G. (2020, 28 January). *The secret gardens of Rohingya refugees.* Equal Times. https://www.equaltimes.org/the-secret-gardens-of-rohingya?lang=en#.YYT oOi-I3s0

Pretari, A. & Anguko, A. (2019). *Livelihoods in South Sudan. Impact evaluation of the "South Sudan Peace and Prosperity Promotion" project.* Effectiveness review series 2016/17. Oxfam GB. https://policy-practice.oxfam.org/resources/livelihoods-in-south-sudan-impact-evaluation-of-the-south-sudan-peace-and-prosp-620864/

Royal Horticultural Society (RHS) (2021). *Transforming lives* [webpage]. https://www.rhs.org.uk/advice/health-and-wellbeing/real-life-stories

SEADS (2021). *Emergency agriculture interventions: Reviewing evidence on the impacts on livelihoods, food security and nutrition.* https://seads-standards.org/wp-content/uploads/2021/04/SEADS_brief1_4.26.21.pdf

Sustainable Food Lab (2016). *Empowering smallholder farmers to improve their incomes.* https://sustainablefoodlab.org/empowering-smallholder-farmers-to-improve-their-incomes/

Woodhill, J., Hasnain, S. & Griffith, A. (2020). *Farmers and food systems: What future for small-scale agriculture?* Environmental Change Institute, University of Oxford. https://www.eci.ox.ac.uk/research/food/downloads/Farming-food-WEB.pdf

World Bank (2012). *Implementation completion and results report for a Zimbabwe emergency agricultural input project.* https://seads-standards.org/wp-content/uploads/2021/04/World-Bank-2012-Zimbabwe.pdf

Chapter 7: Crop-related Infrastructure

CRS (2017). *Guide to facilitating community-led disaster risk management.* CRS. https://www.crs.org/our-work-overseas/research-publications/guide-facilitating-community-led-disaster-risk-management

ICRC (2019). *EcoSec post distribution monitoring report: ILOT – Rehabilitation of rainwater harvesting ponds in Abssan and Khuzaa border areas of Gaza Strip.* ICRC. https://seads-standards.org/wp-content/uploads/2021/04/Asia_06-ICRC-ILOT-Rehabilitation-rainwater.pdf

Marocchino, C. (2009). *A guide to upgrading rural agricultural retail markets.* FAO. http://www.fao.org/docrep/016/ap295e/ap295e.pdf

Mollet, M. (2011). *"Final evaluation results of the 1st and 2nd phase of the EU funded project Restoration and improvement of agriculture based livelihoods and food security for new Internally Displaced Persons (IDP) settlements and returnees in the Area Adjacent to South Ossetia (AASO)"*. Unpublished. FAO.

Muthigani, P., European Committee for Agricultural Training & European Commission (2010). *Manual for investigation, design and rehabilitation of irrigation systems, design manual*. European Committee for Training and Agriculture Somalia. https://agris.fao.org/agris-search/search.do?recordID=SO2005100133

SEADS (2021). *Emergency agriculture interventions: Reviewing evidence on the impacts on livelihoods, food security and nutrition*. SEADS. https://seads-standards .org/wp-content/uploads/2021/04/SEADS_brief1_4.26.21.pdf

Trust Consultancy & Development (2020). *Supporting Syrian refugee families in achieving food security through income-generating vegetable production in Hatay and Midyat (SYR 1052)*. Welt Hunger Hilfe. https://seads-standards.org/wp-content /uploads/2021/04/Trust-Consultancy-and-Dev-2020.pdf

Walter, N., Varela, D.F., Tellez, J. Montoya, A. & Huntington, H. (2017). *Land and rural development programme (LRDP). Mid-term performance evaluation report*. USAID. https://seads-standards.org/wp-content/uploads/2021/04/Walter-et-al.-2017.pdf

Chapter 8: Impact-oriented Monitoring and Evaluation

The Alliance for Child Protection in Humanitarian Action (2020). *Minimum standards for child protection in humanitarian action*. https://alliancecpha.org/sites /default/files/technical/attachments/cpms_2019_final_en.pdf

ALNAP (2016). *Evaluating humanitarian action guide*. ALNAP Guide. London: ALNAP/ODI.

Catley, A., Burns, J., Abebe, D. & Suji, O. (2014). *Participatory impact assessment: A design guide*. Feinstein International Center, Friedman School of Nutrition Science and Policy at Tufts University. https://fic.tufts.edu/publication-item/participatory-impact-assessment-a-design-guide/

Global Food Security Cluster (2022). *Farmers' engagement survey*. Agriculture Working Group. https://fscluster.org/sites/default/files/documents/farmer_engagement_survey_report_final_draft_rev.pdf

Gujit, I. (1998). *Participatory monitoring and impact assessment of sustainable agriculture initiatives: An introduction to the key elements.* SARL Discussion paper no. 1. IIED. https://pubs.iied.org/6139iied

ICRC (2021). *Economic security indicators cookbook.* https://www.icrc.org/en/publication/4505-economic-security-indicators-cookbook

Sapkota, T., Jat, M., Jat, R., Kapoor, P. & Stirling, C. (2016). Yield estimation of food and non-food crops in smallholder production systems. In T.S. Rosenstock, M.C. Rufino, K. Butterbach-Bahl, L. Wollenberg & M. Richards (eds.), *Methods for measuring greenhouse gas balances and evaluating mitigation options in smallholder agriculture* (pp. 163–174). Springer. https://doi.org.10.1007/978-3-319-29794-1

Annex A

FAO (2016). *Seed security assessment: A practitioner's guide.* FAO. https://www.fao.org/plant-treaty/tools/toolbox-for-sustainable-use/details/en/c/1071289/

FAO (2022). Pest and pesticide management. FAO. https://www.fao.org/pest-and-pesticide-management/ipm/integrated-pest-management/en/

IASC (1994). *Definition of complex emergencies.* IASC. https://interagencystanding committee.org/system/files/legacy_files/WG16_4.pdf

Livestock Emergency Guidelines and Standards (LEGS) Project (2014). *Livestock emergency guidelines and standards* (2nd edn.). Practical Action Publishing. http://doi.org/10.3362/9781780448602

United Nations General Assembly (2016). *Report of the open-ended intergovernmental expert working group on indicators and terminology relating to disaster risk reduction.* Seventy-First Session, Item 19(c). A/71/644.

United Nations Office for Disaster Risk Reduction (2015). *Sendai framework for disaster risk reduction 2015–2030.* https://www.preventionweb.net/files/43291_sendaiframeworkfordrren.pdf

Annex B

Grand Bargain Localization Workstream (2020). *Guidance note on humanitarian financing for local actors.* IASC. https://interagencystandingcommittee.org/system/files/2020-05/Guidance%20note%20on%20financing%20May%202020.pdf

Universal Logistics Standards (ULS) (2021). *Universal logistics standards.* https://ul-standards.org/

Annex D: Acknowledgments and Contributors

SEADS steering group

Ugo Bernieri (International Committee of the Red Cross)

Dina Brick (Catholic Relief Services)

Andy Catley (Feinstein International Center, Friedman School of Nutrition Science and Policy at Tufts University)

Salih Abdel Mageed Eldouma (SOS Sahel Sudan)

Ludger Jean Simon (American University of the Caribbean)

Neil Marsland (Food and Agriculture Organization of the United Nations)

Themba Sibanda (Norwegian Refugee Council)

Cathy Watson (Livestock Emergency Guidelines and Standards–LEGS).

Former steering group members

Adam Riddell (World Vision International)

SEADS coordination team

Racey Henderson (Catholic Relief Services)

Anne Radday (Feinstein International Center, Friedman School of Nutrition Science and Policy at Tufts University)

Livestock Emergency Guidelines and Standards–LEGS

The SEADS Project gratefully acknowledges the significant support received from LEGS during the production of the SEADS minimum standards. SEADS has benefited from LEGS' experience and learning, including identifying an evidence base and using a global consultation process.

In addition:

- The structure of SEADS is based on LEGS (2nd edition 2014 and forthcoming 3rd edition).
- Key concepts and tools, including the livelihoods-based approach and livelihood objectives, the decision trees, timing tables, and advantages and disadvantages tables, are taken directly from LEGS.
- The SEADS response-area identification tool (RAIT) is based on the LEGS participatory response identification matrix (PRIM).

Much of the content in Chapters 2, 3, and 4 is drawn directly or adapted from the LEGS 2nd edition Chapter 1: Livestock, Livelihoods and Emergencies, Chapter 2: Core Standards and Cross-Cutting Themes Common to All Livestock Interventions, and Chapter 3: Initial Assessment and Identifying Responses, written by Cathy Watson and Andy Catley.

Donor

The SEADS Project gratefully acknowledges the US Agency for International Development's Bureau for Humanitarian Assistance for their financial support to this project.

SEADS evidence contributors

Interested stakeholders were invited to contribute to the SEADS Project evidence review in 2021. This evidence review formed the basis for the minimum standards in SEADS. A wide range of people, too many to be named here, provided their support and expertise. The SEADS Project gratefully acknowledges all contributors for their valuable inputs.

Chapter contributors

Chapter 1: How to Use this Handbook	Racey Henderson
Chapter 2: The Scope and Approach of SEADS	Racey Henderson and Andy Catley
Chapter 3: SEADS Principles	Racey Henderson, Andy Catley, and Adrian Cullis

Chapter 4: Initial Assessment for Crop-related Crisis Response	Racey Henderson, Andy Catley, and Anne Radday
Chapter 5: Seed and Seed Systems	Louise Sperling with Matthias Mollet, Racey Henderson, and Edward Walters
Chapter 6: Tools, Equipment, and Other Non-seed Inputs	Adrian Cullis
Chapter 7: Crop-related Infrastructure	Isidro Navarro
Chapter 8: Impact-oriented Monitoring and Evaluation	Andy Catley and Stewart Gee

Additional technical support

Shawn McGuire (Food and Agriculture Organization of the United Nations)

Thomas Ølholm (Norwegian Refugee Council)

Matthias Mollet (private consultant)

Field team members

iDE Nepal

ICRC EcoSec Team, Gaza

South Sudan Food Security and Livelihood Cluster

World Vision International—Mozambique

Index

quality of 142
recommended reading on 144
traditional vs. modern 141
training 142, 165
Typhoon Hiyan 21

V

value-chain actors 108
varieties of crops 108, 109

vulnerable groups 41, 63, 177

W

water, access to 36
weather, severe 20
women *see also* vulnerable groups
crops and 58
roles of 41
tool use by 136

www.ingramcontent.com/pod-product-compliance
Lightning Source LLC
Chambersburg PA
CBHW070920030426
42336CB00014BA/2471